"Mixtape Theology captures the heart and soul of the 90s Contemporary Christian Music era, a time that personally resonates with me as it marked the period when I discovered my own calling towards Christian music which eventually led to forming MercyMe. This devotional beautifully weaves together humor, faith, and the music that shaped so many of us."

BART MILLARD - MERCYME

"Point of Grace entered the music scene in the early 90's when Christian music was really ramping up. There were finally outlets for all types of genres of music, but all with the good news of the gospel. Songwriters could actually make a living writing Christian music and we feel we had an opportunity to sing some of those amazing songs. I love the idea of Mixtape Theology! It is definitely the soundtrack to much of my life. Remembering these great songs and having these devotionals that go along with them speaks to my soul."

DENISE JONES - GRAMMY AWARD-NOMINATED AND MULTI DOVE AWARD-WINNING MEMBER OF POINT OF GRACE

"The '90s was a special decade in Christian music. I was honored to be a part of CCM at that time and witness all that God was doing! I love that Mixtape Theology has written a book that draws from the inspiration of that era and brings God's truth to the forefront. Way to go guys!"

REBECCA ST. JAMES

"Oh the 90's CCM era! The most excellent songwriters producing thought provoking lyrics, creative melodies and innovative musicianship. A devotional book like Mixtape Theology will help those who are familiar and unfamiliar with this era, understand and appreciate the inspired meaning of Scripture in song. This book of devotions will plant seeds to drive the reader back the music that God has given for the world to hear. Devotional books have always been my go-to for the short attention span of us creative types and I can't wait to be inspired all over again!"

LISA BEVILL - CCM ARTIST - "TRUE LOVE WAITS" AND "PLACE IN THE SUN" GIRLS CAMP

"When I heard first heard about the *Mixtape Theology* devotional book using 90s CCM as the backdrop, I wasn't sure what to expect. After reading it I am hooked! What a great way to bring these 90s CCM song into the modern age by coupling them with interesting stories, inspiration, and the Word of God!"

DANIELLE KIMMEY TORREZ - OUT OF EDEN

"4HIM's career started in January of 1990, so we had a front row seat to the greatest decade of CCM! Mixtape Theology is not only a gift to those of us who were a part of so many great songs during that era, but also to the listeners who made the journey with us."

ANDY CHRISMAN - 4HIM

MIXTAPE THEOLOGY

90S CHRISTIAN EDITION

A BIBLE STUDY & RETROSPECTIVE INSPIRED BY 90S
CONTEMPORARY CHRISTIAN MUSIC & CULTURE

WILLIAM "ASHLEY" MOFIELD

RACHEL CASH

 NRTBOOKS

A Frank Voice Publishing is the publishing arm of A Frank Voice which seeks to empower Christian authors with the tools and resources to publish their ideas and contribute to the Kingdom of God in a meaningful and inspiring way.

Visit www.afrankvoice.com to learn more.

NRT Books is a novel partnership between A Frank Voice and NewReleaseToday.com. NRT Books is a trusted home for Christian music fans to dive deeper into the Biblical inspirations behind top-selling tracks and to hear from the artists who wrote them while receiving practical life applications around important life themes we all face today.

Find out more at www.NRTBooks.com

Cover & Interior design: Cameron Frank

E-Book ISBN: 978-1-962315-02-9

Paperback ISBN: 978-1-962315-00-5

Hardback ISBN: 978-1-962315-01-2

CONTENTS

THEOLOGY OF SURRENDER:
WHAT IF I STUMBLE?

THEOLOGY OF PRAYER:
GET DOWN.

THEOLOGY OF EVANGELISM:
GO LIGHT YOUR WORLD!

THEOLOGY OF THE HOLY SPIRIT:
HE IS THE LORD OF THE DANCE!

THEOLOGY OF THE NEW HEAVEN & THE NEW EARTH:

IT'S GOLDIE'S LAST DAY.

FOREWORD

BY MAC POWELL OF THIRD DAY

Thank God for Christian music.

I, too, am a 90s CCM kid.

It's not an exaggeration to say that Christian music has changed my life. Growing up in a little town in Alabama, the only Christian music I knew about were songs from the old Baptist hymnal. Every once in a while, the choir would do a cutting-edge Southern Gospel song from Bill Gaither or Dottie Rambo. That was about as "contemporary" as my church music would get.

I moved to Atlanta in 1988. Not long after that, I heard from friends about a rock band called Petra. Even my sister had attended one of their concerts, but I wasn't very interested at the time. Some CCM artists had a couple of pop songs on the radio, like Michael W. Smith and Amy Grant, but that was the extent of my CCM knowledge.

Even though I grew up in church, I wasn't living for Jesus. But in 1991, I started dating a cute, redheaded girl named Aimee (who later became my wife). She started trying to invite me to church with her. She knew I was a big music fan, so she gave me a couple of cassette tapes of Contemporary Christian music to listen to. The first was an album called "Circle Slide" by a cool alternative California band called The Choir.

Even though the lyrics were not overtly Christian, I had heard that the guys in the band were Christians. I couldn't believe that Christians were making such cool music. Then Aimee gave me a cassette of an album called "i 2 (EYE)" by Michael W. Smith. He had a pop hit on the radio called "Place in this World," so I was familiar with him and was excited to hear more of his music. This record opened up my eyes a bit more to contemporary music with a faith message.

I had been in a garage band with a friend of mine from marching band, Mark Lee. Like most high school garage bands, we thought we would take over the world. We weren't that great, but we had lots of hope for what it could turn into.

A month before I was going to graduate from high school, I was feeling a bit lost in life. I had several friends that were encouraging me to grow in my faith, yet I was still trying to do all the things I wanted to do. I needed direction. I needed help. I was lost and didn't know what the future would hold. I was scared of becoming an adult.

Someone at church told me that I should read the book of Romans. I sat on my bed and opened the Table of Contents because I had no idea where the book of Romans was. I found it and turned to Chapter 1. Those pages reminded me of a decision I made as a child to follow Jesus. The words reminded me that God is faithful in keeping His promises, even when we are not. Right then and there, I surrendered to Jesus and asked Him to change my life. I asked Him to help me follow Him and to know Him more.

I went to Mark and told him I was quitting the band. He asked me why, and I explained that I had surrendered to Jesus and wanted to start singing songs about Him. Mark said, "Why don't we start a Christian band?" I didn't really know what that meant, but I was excited about the possibility of a new plan for my life.

Fast forward a couple of months later, I found a *CCM Magazine* in the Christian bookstore. One of the articles was about a band named White

Heart. Mark and I drove to the local record store to see if we could find it. We couldn't find it while sifting through the cassettes, but came across a band called Whitecross. I read the song titles and thought, "I think this might be a Christian record." We bought the tape, hopped in Mark's car, and started listening. We could not believe the sounds that were coming through his speakers. Was *this* Christian music? Could a band rock this hard and be singing about Jesus? I was hooked! I knew I wanted to do that for the rest of my life.

We started with just Mark and me with acoustic guitars. Buying every-thing we could afford, we dove headfirst into the world of Christian music. Not only were we listening to all the Christian music we could find, but we were also going to every Christian concert that came to town.

I had sung the hit song "Awesome God" at church before I knew who Rich Mullins was. As a new CCM fan, I discovered who he was and looked for his albums. "The World As Best As I Remember It, Volume One" had come out, and I didn't think a better record could ever be made. I had to see him live! Thankfully, not too long after that, he did a concert in Atlanta, and I got to meet him face-to-face. That was the first of many memorable times I spent with my writing mentor.

I could go down a long list of records that influenced me, encouraged me in my faith, and helped me to grow in my knowledge of the Word. I could list numerous Christian music concerts by great artists like Newsboys, Audio Adrenaline, dc Talk (who all put out amazing records in the 90s), but I won't bore you too much more with all those details. I'll fast forward a few years into the mid 90s. At that point, Mark and I connected with a couple of other CCM fans. Two of them, David Carr (our drummer) and Tai Anderson (our bass player), joined us in Third Day.

We had been making music together for a year or so when we met Brad Avery, another guitarist who joined the band. We spent countless hours driving across the country in a van and trailer trying to accom-plish what our Christian music heroes were doing.

We wanted simply to grow in our faith, honor God with our lives and music, and bring everyone who listened at least a smaller step closer to Jesus. Concluding with our farewell tour in 2018, we were a band for almost 25 years. Through those amazing years of music and ministry, I remain a huge Christian music fan. Now, as a solo artist that sings songs from back in the day and new ones that I've written, I'm so excited about the new batch of artists who are still encouraging and influencing me. But there's something special about that 90s CCM – how the songs spoke to us, moved our young hearts closer to Jesus, and made us desire to dig deeper into God's Word.

To this day, I still can't believe that I get to share the stage with some of those artists that had such a huge influence on me in the early years, such as Michael W., Newsboys, and my all-time favorite, Steven Curtis Chapman.

This book takes me back and reminds me of why I fell in love with Christian music. This devotional delivers humor, 90s nostalgia, and great memories from those "good old days." Ashley and Rachel will not only bring back the memories of years gone by but will also help you grow in your love for these artists and songs, and even more so, in your love for God and His Word.

PREFACE: WHY 90S CCM?

The memory of when I (Rachel) first heard Contemporary Christian Music (CCM) is still very vivid to me. It was a random summer day in 1993 when our family had just purchased a new CD player. Still a novelty at the time, it was given an entire shelf of importance in our bonus room. Our family CD "collection" included only four discs: Wynonna Judd's debut album, Mariah Carey's MTV Unplugged, the soundtrack from the television sitcom "Dinosaurs" (yes, I'm ashamed), and a hand-me-down Steven Curtis Chapman's *The Great Adventure* album that my aunt said was "not her style."

I had sufficiently worn out Wynonna, Mariah, and the Dinosaurs, and I was a bored 12-year-old on summer break with nothing to do. It was only out of sheer boredom one afternoon that I decided to listen to this discarded CD of an unknown artist, who apparently needed three whole names. I had no idea about the genre of the music, so I had zero expectations. I popped it in, pressed "play," and have been loving it ever since.

Since I (Ashley) am seven years older than Rachel, my journey began not with a CD, but a cassette. After my high school graduation in 1992, my youth pastor presented me with 4HIM's *Face the Nation* on tape. I popped that cassette in and never looked back! After a couple of years of continuous use, the label on my go-to cassette faded, and certain songs could barely play. When I eventually bought my first jam box equipped with a CD player, I upgraded my beloved tape to a CD.

My seminary and ministry journey began around this time, and I began to build my CCM library while diving into theology as well. The collection soon grew to include Steven Curtis Chapman's *The Great Adventure* and Michael W. Smith's *Go West Young Man*, eventually leading to influencers such as Take 6 and Jars of Clay.

What is it about 90s CCM that made such a lasting impact on our lives that we can still remember with clarity the first moments of finding and listening to it? If you bought this book, you likely know exactly how we feel.

This magical combination of excellent music that also celebrated our Savior and inspired us to live for Him spoke straight to our young, zealous hearts. It still does. How can you not be inspired when hearing the Christian life described as "The Great Adventure," complete with horses and trails to blaze, or not be filled with courageous devotion to our Savior when belting out "Jesus Freak"? The biblical truths behind these songs were like newly discovered gold, and the artistry of the music made it fun and exciting to keep digging for more.

Nineties CCM became the living epic soundtrack for our new Christianity. It punctuated important milestones in our lives. These songs provided the mountaintop anthems, the weepy lamentations, and the joy for our journeys. Decades later, we look fondly at this time in our lives and have a deep appreciation for how these songs discipled us and inspired us to know more about this "Awesome God" of the Bible.

INTRODUCTION: HOW TO READ THIS DEVOTIONAL

As you peruse the pages of this book, you'll quickly notice that it's not your typical devotional. This book is a combination of two things–a 90s retrospective and a Bible devotional.

90S CCM RETROSPECTIVE

Throughout the book, you'll find some playful retrospectives on our experiences as 90s CCM kids and young adults. We'll fondly poke fun at some of the decade's clichés and stereotypes while reflecting on the lessons we learned. The best cheese is aged cheese, and we got it.

This book isn't about artist interviews or the story behind the songs. Rather, it's *our* story and *your* story behind the songs and how they shaped us. It's about ordinary people, like you and me, reminiscing about an extraordinary time in our lives.

In addition to good music, cheesy and fun retrospectives, and devotional theology, be prepared for some "comic relief." Enjoy 90s inspired comics by our resident artistic Jesus freak, Liz King.

BIBLE DEVOTIONAL

Listening to 90s CCM takes us back to a time when our faith was new and growing. We were mentored by songwriters who exposed us to significant Christian truths for the first time. Intrigued by what we heard, we looked up the Bible verses that inspired our favorite songs. They served as a springboard for our own personal Bible study. As adults, we want to do that again.

We'll explore theological truths found in some of the most unforgettable 90s CCM songs. Get ready to "Dive" deeper into the biblical passages that correspond with these nostalgic gems and "Walk With the Wise" by exploring what other theologians can contribute to our understanding. We can all do it together as special members of a truly awesome subculture of grown-up 90s kids and young adults.

A list of additional resources for further study is included at the end of each devotion. Some are even free and available in the public domain. Booyah!

Each devotion represents our own meditation and commentary of these beloved tunes and does not necessarily represent the thoughts and views of the artist(s) or songwriter(s). Some might agree with our interpretation, and others might not. We did not consult with the artists and songwriters featured, and none, except for Mac Powell (who wrote the foreword), participated in the writing of this book. Songs were selected based on these criteria:

- **Broad Appeal** - While we love deep cuts, we're "Much Afraid" that not everyone would be thrilled with obscure picks. To fulfill your desire to explore those songs and references that only the most die-hard fans would know, we've created a Deep Cut Scavenger Hunt just for you.
- **Clear Correlation to a Biblical Passage** - We have only chosen songs that have a clear Scriptural reference in the lyrics or specific verses mentioned in the liner notes for the song.
- **Good Hermeneutics** - We've avoided songs that might have an interpretation of the Scripture that we may not agree with or

that discuss a lower-level doctrine that is hotly debated. We are avoiding "I Wish We'd All Been Ready" like the plague.

- **Our Favorites** - Some of the songs were chosen simply because they are our favorites.

As you can imagine, it was difficult to narrow it down to 35 songs. Undoubtedly, we've missed some artists or songs that you love. We apologize for that! Although your favorite may not have been chosen for a devotion, you may still find it referenced somewhere within the book as we reminisce together.

Ready to go to "Another Time, Another Place"? We hope you'll grab your Bible, dust off those new-fangled compact discs and dusty cassettes, and read the song lyrics along with us from your original liner notes just as Family Christian Stores (RIP) and God intended. But, if, like us, you lost them along the way, you can listen to most of these songs for free by scanning the **QR code** below. Saddle up, let's go!

www.mixtapetheology.com / listen

An Open Letter to Those Who Totally Missed the 90s CCM Subculture

Dear Reader,

We understand that the group of people who were part of the 90s CCM subculture is small, and it's possible that you didn't even know it existed. My spouse, for instance, missed out on all of this. While I was jamming to "The Great Adventure" with Steven Curtis Chapman, he was "Under the Table and Dreaming" with Dave Matthews. Many of the puns and inside jokes in this book won't make any sense to him, but that's OK. This book is for everyone.

Here's the truth: While this book features some of our favorite songs from a memorable time in our lives, they are just a means to an end. The goal is to grow in the grace and knowledge of our Lord and Savior Jesus Christ (2 Peter 3:18). His Word is for all of us, regardless of our background or experience.

If you're brave enough to join us 90s CCM kids and young adults, you're welcome here. Please forgive our cheesiness; we promise to ignore your eye rolls. Listen to these songs and study God's truth with us. Our hope is that you'll fall in love with these songs, just as we did, but more importantly, that you'll fall even more deeply in love with God and His Word.

Sincerely,

Rachel Cash, co-author

THEOLOGY OF THE KINGDOM:

MY DELIVERER IS COMING!

LIZ HUMOR

You might be a 90's CCM fan if..

You go to every tent revival, only to be disappointed.

You're a pastor that gets excited when someone screams you're a freak and you think it's a compliment.

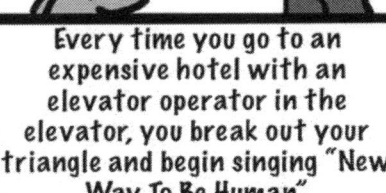

You own a vet clinic and every time a yellow lab dies, you play "Goldie's Last Day" over the intercom.

Every time you go to an expensive hotel with an elevator operator in the elevator, you break out your triangle and begin singing "New Way To Be Human".

You snicker anytime someone says "for him".

You have a colorful collection of vests stashed in your closet.

©Liz King

YOU MIGHT BE A 90S CHRISTIAN IF...

Remember Jeff Foxworthy's hilarious "You might be a redneck if" routine from the 90s? This inspired us. To ready ourselves for our nostalgic ride through 90s Christianity, we reached far back in the memory banks. Prepare to have old memories unlocked. "You might be a 90s Christian if…"

1. You participated in the "interpretive movement." This alternative to dancing for Christians was the perfect loophole for non-movement denominations. Long before Napoleon Dynamite was making bird motions with the Happy Hands Club, Christian youth groups were dancing and carrying Kathy Troccoli's candle to sanctuaries all over America.

2. You boycotted Disney. Jiminy Cricket! What did Mickey ever do to you? Snow White and her brand of debauchery deserve a holy rebuke! Right? I (Ashley) am still a proud member of the denomination who led the boycott; however, I think the words of Steve Urkel are quite appropriate: "Did I do that?"

3. You wore a WWJD bracelet. How could this not be on this list? What a movement! What an idea! What a price! What options! Here is the real question of the decade: "Would Jesus wear a What Would

Jesus Do bracelet?" It makes your brain hurt. Or, would His bracelet say LWID (Look what I did?) or QBBAGTM (Quit buying bracelets and give to missions.)?

4. Your True Love waited. Long before people were kissing dating goodbye, true love was a'waiting. And it was waiting with purity rings, commitment cards, and notes on pretty stationery in bubble cursive with heart-dotted I's crowned by middle school girls. I (Ashley) am forever thankful for this program that became a movement. I still have the purity ring my wife gave me on our wedding night along with the note she wrote to her future husband before she ever knew who that might be. Let's move on to the next one before I start crying sappy, thankful tears like an above-mentioned middle school girl.

5. You rode on a 15-passenger van many times. Because of laws about axles or something, everyone now uses mini buses and bubble buses. But safety wasn't a concern in the 90s. If the air went out, there was sure to be an obnoxious brat to invoke "This is the Song That Never Ends" to help pass the time. For the fringe kids who might be visiting, didn't wear salvation bracelets, or hadn't been through a True Love Waits ceremony, PDA was a common occurrence—and I'm not talking about the Audio Adrenaline kind.

6. You thought the rapture could happen at any minute. With the Y2K apocalypse looming and the popular *Left Behind* book series churning out new releases every 30 minutes, our rapture awareness was strong. Best to always wear clean underwear should they end up in a pile for those left behind to find.

7. You named your pets after your favorite CCM artists. Move over, Beethoven the dog, dc Bark is in the house. Or, perhaps you had three hamsters named Phillips, Craig, and Dean. Maybe a couple of fish named Bebe and Cece? Maybe not. But, now that I mention it, you like the idea. I think every home deserves a Steven Curtis Chapcat, don't you?

8. Your youth group had pre-made matching shirts with pastel colors that stated Christian words such as "Hope" or "Sing." These were great until you got to Kings Island and realized there were three other youth groups present with the same shirt from the same company, and they all rolled their short sleeves too. If you wanted to be slightly cooler, you wore a good parody shirt like "Lord's Gym" or "Jesus is my King" on the Burger King logo. Now that I think about it, I (Ashley) wore a knockoff Reebok logo sweatshirt that said Reeborn in my senior pictures. That was 'da bomb. Add Bugle Boy jeans and Dr. Martens. Ensemble complete.

9. You let your snot run free at the end of a mission trip as "Friends are Friends Forever" played. I know this was the 80s, but the repercussions reached far into the 90s. It's as if a small "friends forever" stone was dropped in a pond, and it rippled and rippled. The tears of those experiences made new ponds for new "friends forever" stones, and the snot flowed freely in youth groups all across our great country.

10. You tried to stay awake during a contemporary service for young people at 8:00 am. Yes, you read that correctly. A contemporary service geared toward "young" people. At. Eight. In. The. Morning. What were they thinking? That makes as much sense as Jerry Falwell's thoughts on the purple Teletubby. We were already sleepy-eyed and we then would repeat "I Could Sing of Your Love Forever" for 12 minutes? Good luck with that. Thankfully, some things evolve for the better, such as Birkenstocks with socks.

11. You witnessed the introduction of a new leadership position in the church—the overhead guy. In conjunction with contemporary music came a new role, and church spiritual gift inventories needed major adjustments. Long before PowerPoint illuminated on a giant screen, the "song leader" projected song lyrics using an old-school "math teacher" overhead projector. This was quite the controversy because the holy hymn books written by the disciples in the first century and donated in memory of Great Aunt Flossie didn't get used. The travesty was real. This new position involving the shifting of transparencies between worship songs required humility, professionalism, coordination, and precision, the likes never witnessed in modern-day ecclesiology.

12. You were in a youth choir. Before praise bands and *Glee,* youth groups had choirs. And the reason you had a choir was to learn a musical complete with synchronized dance moves and props built by the old men of the church and the choir director in his spare time. Our youth group toured the Florida panhandle and held multiple-night performances of *Let's Go to the Rock,* a 50s-based Christian musical that included poodle skirts and malt shops. Al Denson's *The Extra Mile* made the rounds as well as Michael W. Smith's *The Big Picture.* "Cue split-track cassette tape!"

13. You had a Jesus fish on your car. It embodies the American dream that someone somewhere may be rich because they invented the ICTHUS Jesus fish for cars. This is a great idea until someone cuts you off in traffic. Trying to maintain one's witness and not cast off all restraint is too much for any Christian to endure. "What if I Stumble" was written about driving with a Jesus fish, right? To be sure, only real Jesus Freaks were so bold as to attach these plastic beauties to their lowered Honda Civic.

14. You believe there has never ever ever ever ever been a show like *VeggieTales.* One did not have to be a kid to enjoy born again, Jesus-loving vegetables. Whether lookin' for your hairbrush or singing about Mr. Nezzer's bunny, Bob and Larry brought respect to Christian produce everywhere.

15. You got "the talk" from dc Talk. OK, maybe not really. But their songs did unabashedly talk about abstinence and womanly virtue. I (Rachel) remember first learning about Proverbs 31 by its mention in "That Kinda Girl." So, yeah, thanks. That was a decent Christian talk I needed.

How did you do? Do any hit a little too close to home? Start this conversation with some of your old 90s friends, and see what stories you remember together.

"HEAVEN IN THE REAL WORLD"

(1994)

Songwriter: Steven Curtis Chapman

Artist: Steven Curtis Chapman

Album: *Heaven in the Real World*

John 1:14–And the Word became flesh and dwelt among us, and we have seen his glory, glory as of the only Son from the Father, full of grace and truth.

Ephesians 2:12-18–Remember that you were at that time separated from Christ, alienated from the commonwealth of Israel and strangers to the covenants of promise, having no hope and without God in the world. But now in Christ Jesus you who once were far off have been brought near by the blood of Christ. For he himself is our peace, who has made us both one and has broken down in his flesh the dividing wall of hostility by abolishing the law of commandments expressed in ordinances, that he might create in himself one new man in place of the two, so making peace, and might reconcile us both to God in one body through the cross, thereby killing the hostility. And he came and preached peace to you who were far off and peace to those who were near. For through him we both have access in one Spirit to the Father.

90S IMPRESSION

Jesus will fix this messed up and hopeless world.

TODAY'S IMPRESSION

Heaven is God's kingdom, and it is here through Jesus Christ.

Welcome, fellow mixtape theologian! If you are reading this book in order, "Heaven in the Real World" is the first song on our 35-song theological mixtape.

With each song, let the nostalgia run free. Explore old memories and remember how it felt to learn these truths for the first time. Those recollections can be tools that motivate you to explore familiar ideas again with renewed curiosity. Listen to each song along the way. Grab your Bible. Enjoy His presence and His infallible Word, and I promise you'll recapture some of that wonder.

As we continue together, you will be encouraged to consider how your understanding of theological concepts, such as the ones alluded to in these songs, have changed since the 90s. At the top of each devotion, you'll see how our impressions have evolved–sometimes correcting our mistakes, while other times just understanding a little more deeply. Feel free to jot down your own 90s vs Today's Impressions to observe your own growth. You might be surprised at the difference!

If you are new to 90s CCM, welcome to the club. You may not have a 90s impression of these particular songs, and that's totally OK. Just jump in wherever you are!

Ready to dive in and go deep?

Do you remember your first impressions of "Heaven in the Real World"? For me, I heard it from a cassette. I devoured the liner notes and listened to the album in its entirety alone in one sitting. There was just something really captivating about the idea of Jesus being Heaven in the real world.

My understanding of that concept was pretty basic. I was in middle school–young, carefree, and new in the faith. You know what I've learned since those good ol' days? Living in the real world is exhausting. Some days, simply existing feels like a challenge. Like a game of survival of the fittest, it's a dramatic narrative full of conflict. Humanity seems perpetually broken down, worn out, and busted up. "Heaven in the Real World" sits differently as a grown-up, you know?

Not surprising, one of the most appealing aspects of the traditional view of a Christian afterlife (what we might refer to as "Heaven") is that it represents an escape from this world. Instead of despair, in Heaven we have fulfilled hope. Instead of strife, we get eternal peace. Finally, we can rest.

While that is certainly true and worth hoping for, is the Christian life really just about waiting around until the afterlife? Are we just living a long goodbye? Are we stuck in a waiting room until we get called? See ya, wouldn't want to be ya?

I think the good things in Heaven that we look forward to are not just reserved for after death. What about this life? Is it possible for Heaven to be found in the real world?

I still remember the first time I watched the music video for "Heaven in the Real World." In it, we follow a lonely, armor-clad boy who spends his days fighting battles with his sword and shield at the ready. Daily, he walks past a gate where waving children beckon him to join them on the other side.

Finally, one day, it's as if he notices their cries for the first time. He follows them through the gate's old, busted door. He lays down his heavy armor and enjoys freedom in a bright and beautiful Heaven on earth. This simple picture of the gospel–freedom, light, and life in God's presence–brought me to tears.

But that's not the end of the video. The boy doesn't stay there. Exiting through the same door, he steps out again into our world. Changed and clothed in white, he now walks with a mission.

To make sense of this mission, you've got to know what happened to the boy in this story because it's our story, too.

We begin in Eden. It was Heaven in the real world. In *The Unseen Realm*, biblical scholar Michael Heiser observed that Eden was God's holy mountain, the place where both Heaven and Earth came together under God's reign. In Eden, Heaven and Earth were one (See Ezekiel 28:14.).

It was all good in the hood, and God declared it so. Human citizenship in Eden included joyful intimacy with God, meaningful work, and the pleasures of the garden. Eden was a place of life and freedom–because God reigned there. His kingdom rule, not the garden itself, is what made living there Heaven on earth (See Genesis 1:31.).

Alas, Adam and Eve joined forces with an opposing power in Eden to overthrow the rule of the King in His own kingdom. Banished as exiles, they no longer lived in His good kingdom. Humanity forfeited its access to the throne of God and the life and freedom that came with it. We lost Heaven (See Genesis 3:17.).

In Eden, we were free rulers under a glorious King. Outside of it, we become dying slaves to the cruel master of sin (See Ephesians 2:1-3.). Our heart remembers what we had and cries out for what we've lost (See Psalm 84.). ↪This is @ God's tabernacle

God is the only one who can rescue us from the dark domain we now call our real world. However, He saves us not by snatching us into a glorious afterlife, but rather by bringing Heaven to us. His rule and reign returns to Earth through King Jesus.

At just the right time in history, God Himself, our Immanuel, became flesh and dwelt among us. As King, He came to Earth and brought His

?? No one Can take away God's children

kingdom with Him, reclaiming whom and what is rightfully His. Jesus mentioned this reclamation when He prayed, "Your kingdom come, your will be done, on earth as it is in heaven" (Matthew 6:10; see also Genesis 3:15; Matthew 1:23; 3:2; John 1:4-5; 2 Corinthians 8:9.).

Adam and Eve had to leave God's presence, but through Jesus, we are invited back in. Colossians 1:13-14 says it all, "He has delivered us from the domain of darkness and transferred us to the kingdom of his beloved Son, in whom we have redemption, the forgiveness of sins."

Jesus' payment for our sins at the cross rescues us from our lonely exile and returns us to the nearness of God's throne. We are invited to seek His kingdom because it can now be found (See Matthew 6:33; John 10:10; Ephesians 3:11-12; 1 John 2:2.).

Let's go back to the imagery of the "Heaven in the Real World" music video. Remember that busted door that the boy walked through? Jesus is the door and through Him is access to the glorious riches found at His throne. He reigns. We have been rescued. Heavenly citizenship has been reinstated. Through our King, our hope and peace, Heaven is here in the real world for all those who repent and believe (See Mark 1:15; John 10:7; Ephesians 2:4-8; Colossians 1:22.).

Remember the boy who now walked with a mission? Want to know what that mission is? Keep reading. We've got a "New Way to be Human."

- Rachel

REFERENCED VERSES

- Genesis 1:31; 3:15-17
- Psalm 84
- Ezekiel 28:14
- Matthew 1:23; 3:2; 6:10; 6:33; 28:18
- Mark 1:15
- John 1:4-5; 1:14; 8:54; 12:23; 10:7-10
- 2 Corinthians 8:9

- Ephesians 2:1-8; 2:12-18; 3:11-12
- Colossians 1:13-14, 22
- 1 John 2:2

FOR FURTHER STUDY

- *The Day the Revolution Began: Reconsidering the Mission of Jesus's Crucifixion*, N.T. Wright
- *The Unseen Realm: Recovering the Supernatural Worldview of the Bible*, Michael S. Heiser

"NEW WAY TO BE HUMAN"

(1999)

Songwriters: John Foreman and Douglas Kaine McKelvey

Artist: Switchfoot

Album: *New Way to be Human*

John 3:1-6 – Now there was a man of the Pharisees named Nicodemus, a ruler of the Jews. This man came to Jesus by night and said to him, "Rabbi, we know that you are a teacher come from God, for no one can do these signs that you do unless God is with him." Jesus answered him, "Truly, truly, I say to you, unless one is born again he cannot see the kingdom of God." Nicodemus said to him, "How can a man be born when he is old? Can he enter a second time into his mother's womb and be born?" Jesus answered, "Truly, truly, I say to you, unless one is born of water and the Spirit, he cannot enter the kingdom of God. That which is born of the flesh is flesh, and that which is born of the Spirit is spirit.

Romans 6:5-6 – For if we have been united with him in a death like his, we shall certainly be united with him in a resurrection like his. We know that our old self was crucified with him in order that the body of sin might be brought to nothing, so that we would no longer be enslaved to sin.

1 Corinthians 15:20-22 – But in fact Christ has been raised from the dead, the firstfruits of those who have fallen asleep. For as by a man came death, by a man has come also the resurrection of the dead. For as in Adam all die, so also in Christ shall all be made alive.

Ephesians 2:4-7 – But God, being rich in mercy, because of the great love with which he loved us, even when we were dead in our trespasses, made us alive together with Christ—by grace you have been saved—and raised us up with him and seated us with him in the heavenly places in Christ Jesus, so that in the coming ages he might show the immeasurable riches of his grace in kindness toward us in Christ Jesus.

Philippians 3:20-21 – But our citizenship is in heaven, and from it we await a Savior, the Lord Jesus Christ, who will transform our lowly body to be like his glorious body, by the power that enables him even to subject all things to himself.

90S IMPRESSION

As Christians, we need to follow Jesus' example in the way we live.

TODAY'S IMPRESSION

To truly be human and enter into God's kingdom, we must be born again.

Wow, Switchfoot, you're deep. Don't let their cool surfer dude persona fool you. These guys have some profound theological truths in their songs, and "New Way to Be Human" is no exception.

To continue from our "Heaven in the Real World" devotion, we acknowledged that our King has brought His kingdom to us. We were once dying exiles enslaved by sin in the kingdom of darkness, but Jesus' death on the cross rescued us and brought us back into the near-ness of His throne again. For all those who repent and believe, our citizenship in Heaven has been restored. King Jesus accomplishes this through the cross.

You might be thinking, His kingdom is here, so let's go! Last one to the Big House is a rotten egg! Hold up, heavenly citizens. Yes, you have a right to be there, but you aren't ready to walk in. Here's the thing: before you can enter, you must be born again (See John 3:1-8.).

Being born again is a very good thing. In the last devotion, I likened the real world to a survival of the fittest game. Let's continue that anal-ogy. Have you ever seen the show "Naked and Afraid"? These crazy people willingly submit themselves to being stranded in some of the planet's most dangerous environments for 21 days. They can't bring food, water, or even clothes. Many will bow out before they reach Day 21. Those who survive the extreme conditions don't look anything like they did on Day 1. Their bodies are frail and covered in dirt and sores. That's how I imagine us at our point of rescue, but much, much worse.

Totally depraved, we are like walking corpses who are sick, weak, and covered in festering wounds. We crave that which brings our own destruction. We are in no shape to do God's will. Thank God we get to be born again (See 2 Corinthians 5:2.)!

What does being born again mean? When we're born again, we don't become angels or other heavenly beings. We're born again as humans —the humans we were meant to be.

However, it's been a while since we humans were as we were meant to be. For that, we have to go back to Eden where the purpose for Adam and Eve is revealed. There we see that humanity was made in the image of God (See Genesis 1:27.). In *The Unseen Realm*, Old Testament scholar Michael Heiser says that our status as His imagers is what it means to be human. Intertwined, our humanity and His image are forever linked.

This status as His imagers comes with an important role and mission. We are called to be His unique representatives on the Earth. We are to be our King's body and agents. As we do His work and spread the good news of His reign, we participate in His holy restoration project.

When Jesus responded to Nicodemus that we must be born again, He was not saying that we must throw away our humanity. Rather, our humanity needs to be restored. Our self-destructive humanity that is in slavery to sin must die so that we can be reborn into restored humanity that is free from sin to follow the King. As His imagers, we've got kingdom work to do.

Then how do we go about being born again? Just like everything good that is accomplished in us, it is something God does for us. Specifically, Jesus brings about our new birth through His resurrection. *Not everyone, just those that surrender*

With His death, Jesus established His kingdom on earth. With His resurrection, He brought about new life for His followers to live in that kingdom. This mirrors the original Eden story, in which God established His kingdom on Earth and created humanity to live in it. As the firstfruits of this new creation story, the ultimate image bearer, Jesus, is the last Adam and first to experience God's restored kingdom on Earth as a human. As His followers, we, too, will experience God's restored kingdom on Earth as restored humans because we share in His death and resurrection (See 1 Corinthians 15:20-22; Hebrews 1:3.).

When Jesus was made alive again in both spirit and flesh, so were we and so will we be. This is what it means to be born again. Our shared resurrection in Christ allows us to be reborn and live in a way that we were not able to live when we were slaves to sin. When we enter His kingdom, born again, we are now free and alive to glorify our King as His image bearers. This is the only way to be truly human.

-Rachel

REFERENCED VERSES

- Genesis 1:27
- John 3:1-8
- Romans 6:5-6
- 1 Corinthians 15:20-22
- 2 Corinthians 5:2
- Ephesians 2:4-7
- Philippians 3:20-21
- Hebrews 1:3

FOR FURTHER STUDY

- *Being God's Image: Why Creation Still Matters*, Carmen Joy Imes
- *In His Image: 10 Ways God Calls Us to Reflect His Character*, Jen Wilkin
- *Simply Good News: Why the Gospel is News and What Makes it Good*, N.T. Wright
- "The New Humanity," *The Bible Project* (*https://thebibleproject.com/videos/new-humanity/*)

"BIG HOUSE"

(1993)

Songwriters: Barry Blair, Bob Herdman, Will McGinniss, and Mark Stuart

Artist: Audio Adrenaline

Album: *Don't Censor Me*

Exodus 33:13-17–"Now therefore, if I have found favor in your sight, please show me now your ways, that I may know you in order to find favor in your sight. Consider too that this nation is your people." And he said, "My presence will go with you, and I will give you rest." And he said to him, "If your presence will not go with me, do not bring us up from here. For how shall it be known that I have found favor in your sight, I and your people? Is it not in your going with us, so that we are distinct, I and your people, from every other people on the face of the earth?" And the LORD said to Moses, "This very thing that you have spoken I will do, for you have found favor in my sight, and I know you by name."

John 14:1-6–"Let not your hearts be troubled. Believe in God; believe also in me. In my Father's house are many rooms. If it were not so, would I have told you that I go to prepare a place for you? And if I go and prepare a place for you, I will come again and will take you to myself, that where I am you may be also. And you know the way to where I am going." Thomas said to him, "Lord, we do not know where you are going. How can we know the way?" Jesus said to him, "I am the way, and the truth, and the life. No one comes to the Father except through me."

Revelation 3:20–"Behold, I stand at the door and knock. If anyone hears my voice and opens the door, I will come in to him and eat with him, and he with me."

90S IMPRESSION

Someday I get to go to Heaven…and eat, and maybe play football!

TODAY'S IMPRESSION

One of the blessings of this life and the next is my communion with God and fellow believers!

When Rachel and I ventured into writing devotions based on 90s CCM songs, we knew that "Big House" had to be one of our chosen jams. Audio Adrenaline's mega-hit is about as 90s Christian as it comes! The song ranks up there with "Jesus Freak" and "The Great Adventure" as most recognizable to WWJD bracelet-wearing music lovers.

Yet, I have to be honest. When we divvied out who would write about which songs, I was apprehensive when we cast lots and *Big House* landed on me. I thought, "What would Jesus do?" He might not write a devotion about this song.

Don't get me wrong; I like it. The struggle was my understanding of the song. It seems too simplistic. In college, I heard "Big House" and thought it to be a fun song about Heaven. Yeah, maybe we will play football. I like football! We know there will be a feast, and I definitely like to eat. Sure, the yard will be big. Let's sing about it and ask others to go with us! But in my "more theologically mature" grown-up seminary graduate pastoral skin, how could I write a devotion about a song that is more for a 90s VBS puppet show? (Yeah, I saw one.)

Boy, was I wrong.

And thus, the very reason this book of devotions exists. We grow in our faith, and what God teaches is amazing as we grow in Him. Sure, some songs that we loved seem more shallow as the years go by. But the opposite can happen. The song that we thought, even then, was simple, is actually deep.

That is precisely what happened as I began praying, listening, meditating, and studying how to write this devotion. What spiritual depth can I bring to light in a song about playing football in a big, big yard? What is so profound about where you lay your head or when you talk on the phone?

It's there, and I missed it.

The easiest place to start is John 14. As a pastor, I have used this text in numerous funerals. I'm sure I'll continue to do so. Hearing Jesus' words about the place He prepares for us is comforting when a loved one passes. We know death is truly defeated and He will take us to be with Him forever.

Yet, like the song "Big House," there is more in John 14 than meets the eye.

As we discussed in "Heaven in the Real World" and "New Way to Be Human," Jesus our King has established His kingdom on Earth. He invites us to be near Him now. He has made us born again, so that we can glorify Him as King. "Big House" tells the next part of the big, big story–His Church.

In John 14:3, Jesus knew He was about to die. He wanted to comfort His followers. He promised that even though He would be going, He was leaving to prepare a place for them, so that "where I am you may be also."

He called this place "My Father's house." "My Father's house" is also used twice in the Gospel of John. Jesus says it for the first time in 2:16 when He cleanses the temple and refers to it as His Father's house. As He is there, Jesus talks about destroying "this temple," which will rise again in three days. The temple is what He uses to describe Himself. He is a dwelling place of His Father.

This concept is a bit confusing, but Jesus is clear that His body is "the temple." Or perhaps better understood, the temple was a symbol of the incarnated Son of God. Elsewhere in Scripture, we learn that we are His temple (See 1 Corinthians 6:19.)! Or, His houses! Are you starting to see it?

In John 14:3, Jesus reveals that His Father's dwelling has "many mansions." Many translations prefer the word "rooms" instead of "mansions." "Rooms" is a good translation of the Greek word *mone*, and "dwelling places" or "abode" may be the most literal.

To summarize, Jesus is a dwelling place for God, and this dwelling includes many rooms. Interesting.

Where did Jesus go? What preparations did He make? *—a place* He went to the cross! At the cross He prepared a way for our hearts to receive Him. Jesus did what was necessary for us to be His temples. Forgiven and born again, we would become His dwelling place, His many rooms. The Spirit of Christ makes His home in the many hearts of those He redeems! We would be in Him and He in us (See 1 Corinthians 1:27; Galatians 2:20; Ephesians 1-2; Hebrews 10:12-14.).

not sure John 14: 1-6 is talking this.

Remember the 90s worship chorus "Sanctuary?" The place where you worship at church is not "the sanctuary." You are! He prepares us to be His sanctuaries–His house! All together, we are one very big, big house that spans centuries, space, and time.

Mark Stuart talked about the song's inspiration in his autobiography, *Losing My Voice to Find It.* He was in Haiti. He heard the beautiful sound of poor Haitian children singing with joy a song called "Lakay Papa Mwen" ... 'My Father's House.'" The lyrics of the Haitian tune might sound familiar: "Come and go with me to my Father's house. There is joy, joy, joy, In my Father's house." Through a life-changing experience in Haiti, God opened Mark's eyes to the beautiful reality of what he called "finding a key to the backdoor to heaven." (31)

Stuart stated, "It was a song sung by those who still believed that in a fallen world, there was a good Father who had a house big enough to hold their joy" (31). The presence of Jesus is the place where joy becomes a reality. When we house the King of Kings and Lord of Lords, we live with the eternal God indwelling in us, and we will be in His presence for all eternity.

Are there gigantic mansions in Heaven? I have no idea. Is there football? I sure hope so! Here is what I do know, which should bring comfort to each of us, as was intended for those original disciples. We get to experience a deep communion with God in eternity and through our life in the Spirit today! Anyone who trusts in Jesus experiences the truth of being His dwelling place.

The Father's House is in Heaven, and it is also the Church right now, as members of His body become His abode. Trust in Him today. Come, go with me!

-Ashley

REFERENCED VERSES

- Exodus 33:13-17
- John 2:15-17; 14
- 1 Corinthians 1:27; 3:16; 6:19
- Galatians 2:20
- Ephesians 1–2
- Colossians 1:27

- Revelation 3:20

FOR FURTHER STUDY:

- *God Dwells Among Us: A Biblical Theology of the Temple*, G.K. Beale and Mitchell Kim
- *Lifetime Guarantee: Making Your Christian Life Work and What to Do When It Doesn't*, Bill Gillham
- *Losing My Voice to Find It: How a Rockstar Discovered His Greatest Purpose*, Mark Stuart
- *Unseen Realities: Heaven, Hell, Angels and Demons*, R.C. Sproul
- *Until Unity*, Francis Chan

THEOLOGY OF SIN:

GO WEST, YOUNG MAN!

CORNY SONG TO COLORFUL VEST CORRELATION

Abstract from *The Journal of 90s Christian Cheese Science*

Research conducted by: Mixtape Theology Research Institute, Nashville, Tennessee

In the period spanning the early to mid-1990s, Contemporary Christian Music (CCM) bore witness to an eruption of objectively corny musical productions. Meanwhile, audiences experienced a veritable kaleidoscope of very colorful vests, adorning the performers of these corny melodies. Why was corny music often paired with such colorful vests?

Intrigued, the Mixtape Theology Research Institute (MTRI) began to hypothesize that these two seemingly disparate phenomena were, in fact, correlated. Through a rigorous process of scholarly inquiry, our experts are delighted to announce the discovery of the **Corny Song to Colorful Vest Correlation (CSCVC)**: The cornier the song, the more colorful the vest needs to be.

The most salient example of this correlation is exemplified in the case study of Steven Curtis Chapman's objectively very corny "Got to B Tru." During his *Live Adventure* VHS, Mr. Chapman can be seen performing a swift wardrobe change for the corny song. His attire changes from a yellow blazer into a vest featuring a riot of multicolored triangular shapes on the front and bold solid stripes on the back. Immediately after his rendition of the corny piece, he exits the stage to shed the vest, only to reappear clad in the yellow blazer once more. A mere coincidence?

Visualizing the CSCVC using a Venn diagram, we can identify the intersection of the two circles labeled "Corny Song" and "Colorful Vest" as the "Yeah, Bud" Equilibrium, a term coined by the MTRI in reference to our original case study, which initially piqued our interest in this phenomenon.

Fig 1. "Yeah, Bud" Equilibrium

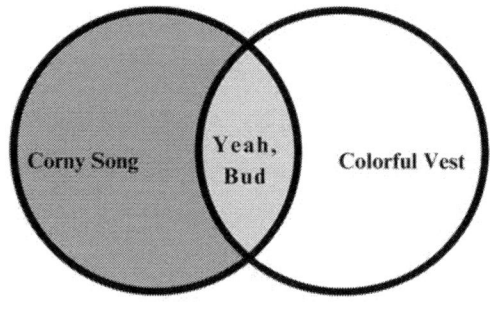

"Yeah, Bud" Equilibrium

When a song or artist falls outside of the "Yeah, Bud" Equilibrium, the audience is thrown into a state of emotional turmoil, wrought with uncertainty and embarrassment as their brains struggle to reconcile conflicting sentiments. However, inside the "Yeah, Bud" Equilibrium, the audience's visceral response is one of unadulterated enjoyment, exuding a sense of playful goofiness and satisfaction. Here, listeners can revel in the unapologetic corniness of the music, safe in the knowledge that the colorful vest bestows upon them permission to let loose and relish the experience.

CORNY SONG TO COLORFUL VEST CORRELATION

One study participant documented his experience with the "Yeah, Bud" Equilibrium as follows:

> I was put in a room alone and made to listen to "Got to B Tru." It was really difficult. Squirming in my chair, I was having secondhand embarrassment the entire time. When the song was over, the investigator entered the room and showed me a tacky, yet colorful, vest. She told me that the performer of the song would be wearing the garment whenever he sang it. She laid the vest on the table before me and played the same song again. While gazing at the vest, it was like a switch had been flipped. I no longer felt awkward and uneasy. The song became a good time, a party for one, and I RSVP'd "yes."

To further illustrate the varying degrees of correlation, we present a sample set of songs and artists ranked on a Likert scale from 1 to 10 and graphed on an XY axis based on their respective ratios. While a 1:1 ratio is rare, it was achieved by none other than Mr. Chapman.

Fig 2. XY Axis

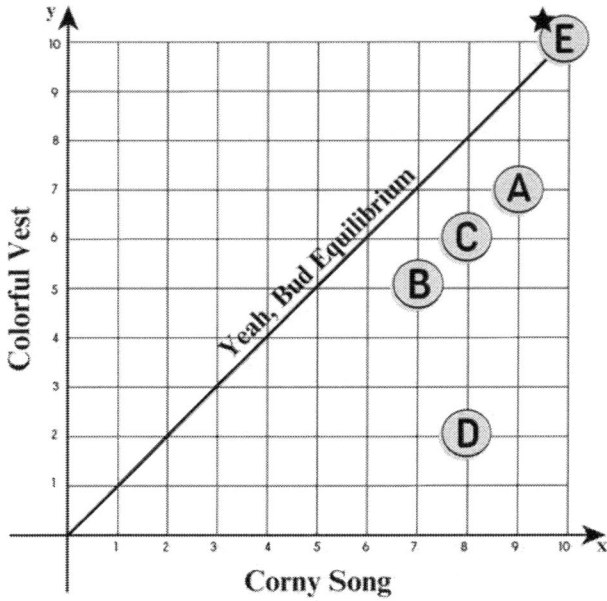

Sample A - "I Luv Rap Music"

Ratio: 9:6
Corny Song: 9
Colorful Vest: 6

In the music video for "I Luv Rap Music," dc Talk's colorful vest wearing is delegated to the dancers, throwing the ratio askew.

Sample B - "Evolution...Redefined"

Ratio: 7:5
Corny Song: 7
Colorful Vest: 5

On the album cover and in the music video, Geoff Moore sports a vest with bold black and white stripes beneath a jacket. While a more subdued example of the colorful vest, it nonetheless fails to achieve the same level of corniness as the theory of evolution.

Sample C - "Picture Perfect"

Ratio: 8:6
Corny Song: 8
Colorful Vest: 6

Michael W. Smith kicked off his 1993 *Change Your World* live tour with the undeniably catchy pop number, "Picture Perfect." In the video, Smitty takes his performance to the next level by wearing a purplish plaid vest under a black jacket. Although the song itself may not earn a high corny rating, his lively dancing during the performance elevates the corniness to an 8. The vest makes a greater impression during his playful, animated choreography. With arms raised in various funky moves, the vest becomes more visible. The innovative utilization of the colorful vest technology is truly remarkable, particularly because it becomes most conspicuous precisely when the audience requires it.

Sample D - "Don't Ya Wanna Rap"

Ratio 8:2
Corny Song: 8
Colorful Vest: 2

On the cusp of the 90s, Bryan Duncan released the music video for his funky song "Don't Ya Wanna Rap," in which he raps most of the lyrics from within a virtual airport. He sports a tasteful black vest with little specks of white, an understated choice that's suitable for a day at the office, but not for a corny song with a rating of 8. The jazz piano is pretty sweet, though.

Sample E - "Got 2 B Tru"

Ratio: 10:10 or 1 (the perfect "Yeah, Bud" Equilibrium)
Corny Song: 10
Colorful Vest: 10

As previously mentioned, the CSCVC is evident in "Got 2 B Tru." This pseudo-rap song's 10:10 ratio of corniness to colorful vest perfectly illustrates the Equilibrium of "Yeah, Bud" and displays the artist's concern for his audience's entertainment.

If you've also observed this correlation between corny songs and colorful vests, share your findings with us at *mixtapetheology.com*.

"MORE THAN YOU KNOW"

(1996)

Songwriters: Michael Bragg, Todd Collins, and Lisa Kimmey Winans

Artist: Out of Eden

Album: *More Than You Know*

Romans 8:38-39–For I am sure that neither death nor life, nor angels nor rulers, nor things present nor things to come, nor powers, nor height nor depth, nor anything else in all creation, will be able to separate us from the love of God in Christ Jesus our Lord.

Ephesians 3:17-19–so that Christ may dwell in your hearts through faith—that you, being rooted and grounded in love, may have strength to comprehend with all the saints what is the breadth and length and height and depth, and to know the love of Christ that surpasses knowledge, that you may be filled with all the fullness of God.

90S IMPRESSION

God loves me more than I can know.

TODAY'S IMPRESSION

Yes, God loves me more than I can comprehend with my mind alone. I need faith to know that love.

In 1994, still very new to Christian music, my parents purchased third-row seats for us to attend dc Talk's *Free at Last* tour in Nashville. Epic parenting. While this wasn't my first concert, it was the first concert of my choosing. I chose wisely.

The opening act for dc Talk was this brand new group of three sisters–Out of Eden. Decked out in plaid baby-doll dresses, this young teenage trio knocked my socks off. Subsequently, their albums would play on repeat throughout my middle and high school years, and when I was alone, I was the off-key fourth member of Out of Eden.

"More Than You Know" is the title track from their second album. This album speaks to listeners who may be on a search for something meaningful. The songs inspire them to discover their heart's desires through the love of a compassionate Father, who cares for them more than they could ever know. These lyrics said all the things that I wanted to say to my young peers around me that were lost and hurting.

In the words of the great theologians dc Talk, we just "wanna be loved." It's true. We were designed to love and to be loved. In Ephesians, Paul prayed that believers would know God's love,

> ...so that Christ may dwell in your hearts through faith–that you, being rooted and grounded in love, may have strength to comprehend with all the saints what is the breadth and length and height and depth, and to know the love of Christ that

surpasses knowledge, that you may be filled with all the fullness of God (3:17-19).

His love is more than we could possibly comprehend, yet Paul wanted believers to know it. How is this possible?

Our minds alone can't fathom such love, even so, we are invited to comprehend it.

To be honest, I struggle with the magnitude of God's love for me. Do you? At times, my sin just seems so great that it's easy to doubt that God would still love me. Maybe you have experienced that same doubt and guilt that comes along with acknowledging your own sin. Flashes of my past indiscretions replay like a movie in my mind. We have a choice when we repent–to hide in shame or to embrace being rooted and grounded in His love. Paul made it clear which is the better choice. Choose wisely.

How then can we be rooted and grounded in God's love? Knowing God's love is not merely an intellectual exercise, it's a spiritual one. In his book *Trusting God*, Jerry Bridges wrote,

> God's unfailing love for us is an objective fact affirmed over and over in the Scriptures. It is true whether we believe it or not. Our doubts do not destroy God's love, nor does our faith create it. It originates in the very nature of God, who is love, and it flows to us through our union with His beloved Son. But the experience of that love and the comfort it is intended to bring is dependent upon our believing the truth about God's love as it is revealed in Scriptures. (295)

It takes the gift of faith to believe the incredible truth of God's love. As the song entreats, we have to open our spiritual eyes to see and believe.

What is the truth about God's love? We believe that Jesus is the ultimate outpouring of God's love (See John 15:13.). Even as sinners, He died for us (See Romans 5:8.). As His own, we are in Him and He is in us (See 1 Corinthians 6:19-20.). Because we exist in Him, we will never be deprived of God's limitless love. This is why Paul confidently said,

> For I am sure that neither death nor life, nor angels nor rulers, nor things present nor things to come, nor powers, nor height nor depth, nor anything else in all creation, will be able to separate us from the love of God in Christ Jesus our Lord (Romans 8:38-39).

A world without the spiritual means to comprehend God's love will naturally reject it. God's love is replaced with shallow self-affirming and pseudo-uplifting messages, such as "I am Enough." I have a very godly friend that had a decorative print with that popular motto in her home. In a moment of God-given clarity during a challenging time, my friend realized that the print should say, "The I AM is enough." We find that God, The I AM, is enough to be all you need to satisfy your deepest longing to be loved. Don't let the world fool you into a shallow substitution.

It's natural to have doubts and moments of weakness. In these times, perhaps the right question isn't "Am I enough?" but rather "Is Jesus enough?" Don't look in the mirror for this answer. Look at the cross. Didn't Jesus prove God's love for you? Yes! Certainty of God's love won't be found in yourself but rather in Jesus and what He did for you (See John 3:16.).

Knowing that God loves you isn't just so you'll feel good, and it does! Did you know that experiencing God's love for you is essential to following Him? Rooted and grounded in His love, you'll know that love can't be found in all the wrong places. His love will fill you with the fullness of His presence while motivating you to love Him and to love others as He has loved you (See 1 John 4:19.). Obedience without love is merely works-based religion and legalism (See 1 Corinthians 13:1-3.).

If this is something you struggle with, come join me. Put yourself in Paul's prayer that you would be deeply rooted and grounded in His love. Ask Him to increase your faith in this area for His purposes and glory. He wants this for you. In Jesus, you are invited to scale the depths of the breadth and length and height of God's love. Look at the cross. He loves you more than you could ever know.

-Rachel

REFERENCED VERSES

- John 3:16; 15:13
- Romans 5:8; 8:38-39
- 1 Corinthians 6:19-20; 13:1-3
- Ephesians 3:17-19
- 1 John 4:19

FOR FURTHER STUDY

- *No Greater Love: Experiencing the Heart of Jesus through the Gospel of John*, A.W. Tozer
- *The Ragamuffin Gospel: Good News for the Bedraggled, Beat-Up and Burnt Out*, Brennan Manning
- *Trusting God*, Jerry Bridges

"THE DEVIL IS BAD"

(1998)

Songwriters: Bret Barker, James Charles Carter, Todd Gruener, Valentine Eugene Hellman, Brian Christopher Morris, and Andrew Schar

Artist: The W's

Album: *Fourth from the Last*

Genesis 3:1-5–Now the serpent was more crafty than any other beast of the field that the LORD God had made. He said to the woman, "Did God actually say, 'You shall not eat of any tree in the garden'?" And the woman said to the serpent, "We may eat of the fruit of the trees in the garden, but God said, 'You shall not eat of the fruit of the tree that is in the midst of the garden, neither shall you touch it, lest you die.'" But the serpent said to the woman, "You will not surely die. For God knows that when you eat of it your eyes will be opened, and you will be like God, knowing good and evil."

Matthew 4:1-10–Then Jesus was led up by the Spirit into the wilderness to be tempted by the devil. And after fasting forty days and forty nights, he was hungry. And the tempter came and said to him, "If you are the Son of God, command these stones to become loaves of bread." But he answered, "It is written, "'Man shall not live by bread alone, but by every word that comes from the mouth of God.'"

Then the devil took him to the holy city and set him on the pinnacle of the temple and said to him, "If you are the Son of God, throw yourself down, for it is written, "'He will command his angels concerning you,' and "'On their hands they will bear you up, lest you strike your foot against a stone.'"

Jesus said to him, "Again it is written, 'You shall not put the Lord your God to the test.'" Again, the devil took him to a very high mountain and showed him all the kingdoms of the world and their glory. And he said to him, "All these I will give you, if you will fall down and worship me." Then Jesus said to him, "Be gone, Satan! For it is written, "'You shall worship the Lord your God and him only shall you serve.'"

90S IMPRESSION

The devil is bad and tempts us to do things we aren't supposed to do.

TODAY'S IMPRESSION

The devil's temptation is all about idolatry. He wants us to lose our trust in God and usurp God's authority and rightful place in our lives as the source of all we need.

The 90s CCM scene was not only about inspiring faith and worship, but also about letting loose and having a blast! Ska bands like The W's, Supertones, and Five Iron Frenzy were instant favorites among young CCM enthusiasts for their energetic and upbeat vibes. The W's "The

Devil is Bad" is a true testament to the fun and lively spirit that defined the era.

The devil, the main character of this bouncy tune, is indeed bad, to say the least. He goes by a lot of names, none of which are good–Satan, the devil, Serpent, Evil One…

What exactly makes the devil so bad? I would summarize it as this: The devil is obsessed with idolatrous self-worship. It's his weapon and his goal. While there is a lot of mystery that surrounds this character (such as where he came from and what/who exactly he is), his modus operandi is clear. Everything he does is focused on kicking God off His throne and placing himself there instead: idolatry.

In today's post-modern culture, idolatry is not always a stereotypical worship of a golden calf idol. In *Equipped to Love*, Norm Wakefield described what idolatry is, and to me, it looks exactly like what the devil does.

> When we look to a creature, an object, or an idea to be the source of provision, comfort, happiness, or power, we are worshiping an idol. Someone under the influence of the spirit of idolatry seeks to fashion the person or situation to supply self-centered desires and comfort. (26)

To see the very first appearance of the adversary in action, we need to go back to the garden of Eden. In Genesis 3, we can see how the evil one began his attack on Eve with a leading question –a question meant to cast doubt rather than genuinely seek information. "Did God actually say…?" Then he confirmed her doubts with a bold-faced lie. "You shall not…" Why? He wanted her whole view of God to become corrupted so that she would begin to believe that God was untrustworthy and holding back something good that she should have.

Wow. He just attempted character assassination on God. Satan goes straight for the jugular here by having Eve question God's legitimacy as King. Perhaps she and Adam would be the better choice for deciding what is best for them? That is the temptation that draws her in and ensnares them both. In *Even Better than Eden*, Nancy Guthrie said it like this,

> To eat of it was to assume the right to decide for oneself what is good and what is evil rather than depend on God to define good and evil. This prohibition was essentially a call to faith, a call to let God be God rather than usurp His authority. (33)

But we commit an epic fail. As image bearers, we fail at our vocation. Through an evil coup involving a serpent and a piece of fruit, humanity has attempted to make ourselves into our own illegitimate gods. Idolatry is both an assault on God's character and our true humanity as image bearers, and that's why Satan is focused on this as his weapon of choice.

While Adam, Eve, and the rest of us spectacularly fail at our attempts to be a perfect image bearer, Jesus, the last Adam, does not. During Jesus' 40-day/night fasting and testing in the wilderness, Satan waved that same old forbidden fruit of idolatry in Jesus' face. This account, both in Matthew 4 and Luke 4, shows us Satan's three failed attempts to get Jesus to commit idolatry and rebel against the King as Adam did.

As observers, this gives us a unique chance to watch Satan go all out to defeat THE Son of Man. Satan has gotta go big or go home. This is for all the pitchforks.

What does Jesus do to combat Satan's best shot? He trusts in God's character. His trust in the goodness and wisdom of God never falters! The very Word of God is all Jesus needs to overcome. Jesus remains true to His purpose to embody God's will above all else.

Satan can just skiddly-doo his way over to the loser's corner (h-e-double hockey sticks).

Let's strip away the illusion of what the devil's temptations are truly all about. Temptations begin with character assassination of God whereby we are tempted to usurp His authority for ourselves–the old snatch and grab. Sin becomes our chosen method for fulfilling our desires outside of God's will. Whether your specific sin is to lie, steal, murder, lust, and so forth, the root of them all is the same—idolatry.

When described on a page, sin seems so easy to spot from a mile away; but looks can be deceiving. Modern-day platitudes, such as: "You are enough," "Follow your heart," and "Find your truth," are just a few examples of idolatry hiding in plain sight. Be on guard, as the devil is truly a slithering snake in the grass.

Seeking to honor and glorify the King as His human image-bearers is what the Christian life is all about. Although we failed as humanity, Jesus succeeded. Through Jesus, the perfect Image Bearer, we have the ultimate victory over the devil. God can grant us repentance and still use our mistakes for His glory and our sanctification.

Yeah, the devil is indeed bad, but God is good. (Hey!)

- Rachel

REFERENCED VERSES

- Genesis 3:1-5
- Matthew 4:1-10
- Luke 4

FOR FURTHER STUDY

- *Awake & Alive to Truth: Finding Truth in the Chaos of a Relativistic World*, John L. Cooper
- *Equipped to Love: Building Idolatry-Free Relationships*, Norm Wakefield
- *Even Better than Eden: Nine Ways the Bible's Story Changes Everything About Your Story*, Nancy Guthrie
- *Live Your Truth and Other Lies: Exposing Popular Deceptions that Make Us Anxious, Exhausted, and Self-Obsessed*, Alisa Childers

"HOLD ME JESUS"

(1993)

Songwriter: Rich Mullins

Artist: Rich Mullins

Album: *A Liturgy, a Legacy, and a Ragamuffin Band*

1 Corinthians 10:13–No temptation has overtaken you that is not common to man. God is faithful, and he will not let you be tempted beyond your ability, but with the temptation he will also provide the way of escape, that you may be able to endure it.

Galatians 5:16-18–But I say, walk by the Spirit, and you will not gratify the desires of the flesh. For the desires of the flesh are against the Spirit, and the desires of the Spirit are against the flesh, for these are opposed to each other, to keep you from doing the things you want to do. But if you are led by the Spirit, you are not under the law.

1 Peter 5:6-7–Humble yourselves, therefore, under the mighty hand of God so that at the proper time he may exalt you, casting all your anxieties on him, because he cares for you.

90S IMPRESSION

When I am struggling or scared, I need Jesus to hold me.

TODAY'S IMPRESSION

Often the greatest obstacle a Christian faces is temptation. Thankfully, it is not the size of my willpower or the level I perform that brings victory. I overcome as I surrender to the Spirit, who gives me life.

"Hold Me Jesus" is a brutally honest song to which we all relate but are reluctant to admit. Most people read the title or hear the lyrics and assume it is about fear when it is actually about temptation. And again, it is honest.

For Christians, transparency seems to be diverted at all costs when revealing the struggle of temptation. No one likes to open up their souls and allow others to view where they fall short. In temptation, we prefer not to confess that we are failing and struggling to find victory. We do not like to put ourselves out there.

Rich Mullins does precisely that. He puts himself out there. This song has always been one of my favorites, yet I failed to see its brutal honesty regarding temptation. We can all relate, and each faces battles and sinful cravings. What are we to do when faced with temptation?

As the common catchphrase goes, the struggle is real. Honest confession and surrender are the starting places. We must be willing to confess that, as Kris Lundgaard states in *The Enemy Within*, "Our hearts are a maze that only God can solve." (36)

The apostle Paul expressed the reality of the struggle in Galatians 5:16-18, and to paraphrase, he essentially stated: "I'm a Christian now. Why am I still fighting a battle with my flesh? As soon as I seem to do well, I fall on my face once again."

The flesh and the Spirit are in complete opposition to one another and cannot cooperate. Jesus reminded His disciples, "Watch and pray that you may not enter into temptation. The spirit indeed is willing, but the flesh is weak" (Matthew 26:41). This struggle is ongoing and inevitable until we see Jesus face-to-face. The conflict within each of us seeks to pull us away from the very place where Christ came to bring peace—our hearts.

Often believers reason that once they come to Christ, all of their problems are over. To use a 90s phrase, "Whatever!" How very wrong is that idea! Problems exist. And when you wake up tomorrow, new difficulties and temptations will be waiting to bring the old some company.

Consider the honesty of "Hold Me Jesus." Mullins was transparent in admitting that life is confusing, and often the obstacles seem larger than our faith. We tend to feel lost in darkness, so much to the point of feeling numb. I recall the famous Christian singer Keith Green toiling over the same idea, and he wished for God to make his heart have baby skin again because it was calloused.

Surrender challenges us in our flesh. Our only hope is to fall to our knees and ask the God of all creation to hold and heal us. In our fear and temptation, faith is the victory.

Have you ever lifted something heavy and tried to hold it up for an extended time? Your muscles eventually give way. Either what you are holding will fall or you will fall. You understand this analogy well if you have ever done any weight lifting or working out. At a certain point, you cannot push the weights up any longer, and your muscles begin to quiver and shriek in exhaustion. Sooner or later, something has to give.

Of course, those same muscles show up a couple of days later and go through this same routine: another day and another weightlifting session. And to be sure, the same results. You will get to the point where you will not be able to lift much of anything, or you will drop.

Similarly, this is how we try to overcome temptation. We try to do the heavy lifting and do it repeatedly. This struggle is not what Jesus has planned for us as our means to overcome temptation, from one shaky lifting session to the next.

A better way exists.

The better way is falling down and admitting we are unable. The better way is not a *way*, but a *Person*! The person is the Spirit of God. In the confusion and numbness of temptation, we have hope. Even if my flesh presents challenges, Christ in me, the hope of glory, is up for the challenge.

And as deflating as the flesh can be, do not lose heart. Inner conflict is a testimony that you are His. It is a red flag warning that a better way exists, and by the Spirit, you can walk in it. Remember who you are and that the power of sin no longer has control of you. Raise your arms in surrender and remember what He has done. It is not even the size of your faith. Ultimately, it boils down to where you place your faith. Is it in God Almighty? That makes all the difference. Confess, surrender, and trust.

The Spirit reminds us that we are not powerful enough to overcome temptation, so we must trust in Him! Our flesh and willpower will never win the battle that rages, and our performance will never be impressive enough to scare sin away.

In "Hold Me Jesus," Rich Mullins heard a hymn played by a Salvation Army band. The lyrics do not mention the hymn's name, but it seems to be a reminder. The familiar tune speaks of grace. Whatever this hymn might be, its words remind the sufferer of the grace of God that sustains us in this battle. When we hear and embrace the hymn of grace, our flesh gives way to our lifeline—God's grace.

What a fantastic theological concept! God's grace is more powerful than our resistance to it. His grace is more powerful than anything we can muster, so we trust. Temptation and sin are powerful. Jesus in us is more powerful.

The apostle Paul reminded us in 1 Corinthians 10:13 that no temptation exists that can overtake us. God provides a way out, and the way He provides is His Son and His Spirit within.

Temptation and struggling with sin indeed ravage us. To be clear, when we see our sin, we should hate it. And when faced with temptation, we should trust the more immense power at work. When we see our Savior, we embrace Him as He embraces us. He is there and desires to provide the way out that we may be able to endure. As Andrew Farley so eloquently put it, "With awareness of his unconditional presence comes the power to say no to sin." (*The Naked Gospel*, 205)

Are you shaking like a leaf? Be encouraged because you are not alone. The temptations and struggles of the windstorms of life knock us to our knees.

Thankfully, on our knees is the best place to be in our time of need! God's grace will hold us tight as He wraps us in His arms. When temptation knocks on the door, by faith, let the Spirit answer. Cast all your cares on Him, for He cares for you (See 1 Peter 5:7.).

Jesus is our King of Glory. He is the Prince of Peace!

- Ashley

REFERENCED VERSES

- Isaiah 9:6
- Matthew 26:41
- 1 Corinthians 2:8; 10:31
- Galatians 5:16-18
- Colossians 1:27
- 1 Peter 5:6-7

FOR FURTHER STUDY

- *The Enemy Within: Straight Talk About the Power and Defeat of Sin,* Kris A. Lundgaard
- *The Naked Gospel: The Truth You May Never Hear in Church,* Andrew Farley
- *The Screwtape Letters,* C.S. Lewis

"LIQUID"

(1995)

Songwriters: Jars of Clay (lyrics by Dan Haseltine)

Artist: Jars of Clay

Album: *Jars of Clay*

Romans 3:21-25–But now the righteousness of God has been manifested apart from the law, although the Law and the Prophets bear witness to it–the righteousness of God through faith in Jesus Christ for all who believe. For there is no distinction: for all have sinned and fall short of the glory of God, and are justified by his grace as a gift, through the redemption that is in Christ Jesus, whom God put forward as a propitiation by his blood, to be received by faith.

1 Corinthians 2:1-2–And I, when I came to you, brothers, did not come proclaiming to you the testimony of God with lofty speech or wisdom. For I decided to know nothing among you except Jesus Christ and him crucified.

Galatians 2:21–I do not nullify the grace of God, for if righteousness were through the law, then Christ died for no purpose.

90S IMPRESSION

Jesus didn't die for nothing.

TODAY'S IMPRESSION

Jesus' blood is essential for my salvation. As a top-tier doctrine, Jesus and His work on the cross should be our focus.

In 1995, Jars of Clay released their first album and immediately cemented themselves as one of the "cool kids" of the 90s Christian music scene. Played on "secular" radio stations, the band crossed genre boundaries not often traversed by Christian artists.

Decades later, this debut album still holds up, and I admire its musical creativity and lyrical vulnerability even more as an adult. The album begins with the unforgettable song, "Liquid." Within the first few moments, it captures your attention. Violins, acoustic guitars, Gregorian chants...let's go! The lyrics are simple and effective: Jesus' blood wasn't shed for nothing. It's a supreme doctrine in a single line.

The English Standard Version (ESV) contains over 300 verses that mention blood. From the first animal sacrifice to cover the nakedness of Adam and Eve in Genesis to the blood-stained Lamb in Revelation, blood's role in our salvation is key to our understanding of how our salvation is achieved. Verse after verse, the Bible makes one message loud and clear: Jesus' voluntary sacrifice secures our salvation and all the blessings that come with it. He is our one and only Savior. We are the reason He chose to die.

The doctrine of Jesus' blood to reconcile us to God is a non-negotiable tenant of Christianity. Romans 3:21-25 is one of the many proof texts for this belief.

> But now the righteousness of God has been manifested apart from the law, although the Law and the Prophets bear witness to it–the righteousness of God through faith in Jesus Christ for all who believe. For there is no distinction: for all have sinned and fall short of the glory of God, and are justified by his grace as a gift, through the redemption that is in Christ Jesus, whom God put forward as a propitiation by his blood, to be received by faith.

That word "propitiation" speaks of bringing reconciliation through a pardon. Jesus paid our penalty with His blood on the cross, which makes our pardon possible. Although in many ways this is a mysterious teaching to us, through faith, we know and believe this is how God chose to save us.

A "gospel message" that removes the necessity and supremacy of Jesus' sacrifice on the cross for our sin is a false gospel to be sure. For some, this false gospel is the message of "Christianity" they were taught in the 90s.

While Dr. Ashley and I smile and fondly remember the Christianity of our youth, not everyone who grew up in 90s Christian culture walked away with a flood of nostalgic warm fuzzies. Some were abused or left traumatized by sinful leadership. Some, anxious and doubting, were admonished to simply "have more faith." When struggling with sin, others were judged and shamed instead of loved and discipled. In some churches, God's grace was replaced with man's legalism, an empty fundamentalism where the blood of Christ has no power to forgive, cleanse, or sanctify.

The wounds are real and some are very deep. It's no wonder that the songs and memories we hold dear can instead be cruel reminders of a time they don't wish to revisit. We acknowledge those individuals, and we grieve with them. We wish nothing more than for God to redeem the pain, heal what is broken, and bless them with their own love song for a Savior.

Combine a legalistic, works-based gospel with church hypocrisy, and you've got a roadmap for leaving the faith. For the sake of ourselves and others, we must examine past and present theology to ensure that the gospel we live, preach, and trust is all about Christ and Him crucified. As Paul taught,

> And I, when I came to you, brothers, did not come proclaiming to you the testimony of God with lofty speech or wisdom. For I decided to know nothing among you except Jesus Christ and him crucified (1 Corinthians 2:1-2).

Let's practice that self-examination together with a quintessential 90s Christian experience, the purity movement. Let's ask ourselves if our participation emulated Paul's singular focus.

The purity movement is perhaps one of the most debated aspects of 90s Christian youth group culture. This movement, sometimes called True Love Waits, Raise the Roof, or any other number of names, encouraged youth to stay abstinent until marriage. At rallies and ceremonies, youth were encouraged to sign a sexual purity pledge card or wear a purity ring to signify their commitment to wait.

A low-hanging fruit ripe for criticism, it's been picked apart by Christians and non-Christians alike. As our King's ambassadors, we must examine what went right and what went wrong. We do this not out of anger or hostility but rather for genuine care and love for His Church and kingdom. We should want to get this right.

If you participated in purity culture, what was your experience? Do you notice any lingering doctrines about God that you realize now aren't biblical? For me, a natural rule follower, purity culture gave me a sense of pride and self-righteousness that were undeserved. The glittering gold of my purity ring blinded me from seeing my true state before a holy God. Arrogantly, I equated sexual purity with being right with God.

Being right with God is accomplished through Jesus' blood alone. In *Talking Back to Purity Culture*, author Rachel Joy Welcher lamented, "So many of us walked right past the gospel on our way to a purity conference." (137) Can I get a witness?

Imagine if the movement had taught sexual purity in this way (in Welcher's words),

> God's sexual ethic is first meant to reveal our sin as 'utterly sinful' (Romans 7:13) and to devastate us into acknowledging our need for a Savior. Jesus' Sermon on the Mount reveals us all as sexual sinners: the virgins, the serial adulterers, the porn addicts. We all fall short of God's command to see one another as brothers and sisters in all purity. The main point is not pursuing sexual purity but recognizing our impurity and our desperate need for Christ. (137)

Imagine if this is what most teens walked away understanding about true purity, which extends far beyond the sexual realm. Recasting purity in the light of the cross makes all the difference. The message changes from "If you want to be pure, you need this purity pledge," to "If you want to be pure, you need the cross."

By His grace, He teaches me that righteousness *and* purity come from Christ alone, not in my own works. So it is for everyone. Whether we kept our purity pledge or not, we are all sinners and must depend on the blood of Christ to cleanse us from all sin (See Hebrews 9:14.).

In many ways, True Love Waits-like programs benefitted me. It taught me that God created sex to be within the boundaries of faithful marriage. In a world that screams the opposite, this is a much-needed and important teaching that the Church should not abandon. But in some ways, by isolating the one sin of premarital sex from all others, the movement missed the mark for me. My only wish is that I would have looked to Jesus alone for true purity and righteousness rather than an abstinence commitment card.

My experience is only one of many. Perhaps your experience in the purity movement included the more important gospel message and you were led to the cross. If so, what a blessing! As you examine your own past 90s Christian experiences, ask that God would show you where, if any, Jesus' sacrifice was not the paramount teaching. Like our example from purity culture, how would the message be different if the focus was on the necessity of the cross?

Although He never changes, our understanding of God will continue to evolve as we grow older. Maybe years from now, we will have the wisdom to spot where we might be in error today. New movements and programs in the church will come and go, surely influencing us along the way. We shouldn't be afraid to stop and examine them with Scripture.

Is Christ and Him crucified the centerpiece of the message or does it miss the main point? Let the doctrine of Jesus' blood be your northern star as you navigate.

Will we be humble enough to respond to His correction? Much is at stake if we choose to ignore it. With His Spirit, we can repent, learn, and gain wisdom.

Even still, on this side of the New Heaven and the New Earth, we will never get all theology completely right or know it all for certain. I believe what the song's lyricist proclaims. There is indeed one thing that I know and you can know: our broken and blood-stained Jesus did not die for nothing. His blood accomplished what nothing and no one else could ever begin to attempt: our salvation and all the glorious blessings that follow. No movement, no political ideology, and no human work are more important than that. No other message should take its place as supreme. His shed blood is the gospel of the glory of Christ, our treasure in jars of clay (See 2 Corinthians 4:4-7.). Indeed, His death wasn't for nothing.

- Rachel

REFERENCED VERSES

- Romans 3:21-25; 7:13
- 1 Corinthians 2:1-2
- 2 Corinthians 4:4-7
- Galatians 2:21
- Hebrews 9:14

FOR FURTHER STUDY

- *Hymns of the Son: The Trinity Project: Book 1*, Cameron Frank, Preston Norman, and Nathan Drake
- *Talking Back to Purity Culture: Rediscovering Faithful Christian Sexuality*, Rachel Joy Welcher
- *The Thrill of Orthodoxy: Rediscovering the Adventure of Christian Faith*, Trevin Wax

THEOLOGY OF SALVATION:

WHAT DID JESUS DO?

RIGHTEOUS STYLE OF THE 90S CCM YOUNG PERSON

Do you remember the 90s Christian kid wardrobe? It was so iconic that even now, years later, we can't help but laugh (and cringe) at the fashion choices we made. To show off your faith back then, you needed only three things:

1. WWJD bracelet
2. Logo rip-off shirt (for example, "Spirit" instead of "Sprite")
3. Purity Ring

Let's dive deeper into each one, shall we?

1. WWJD BRACELET

Did you know that "What Would Jesus Do?" is actually from an 1896 book called *In His Steps: What Would Jesus Do?* by Charles Sheldon? WWJD was a double 90s phenomenon, popular in both the 1890s and the 1990s. That's pretty impressive! What's even more impressive is the plethora of colors that you could find for these scrappy little bracelets. Because they were so cheap, you could fancy yourself one in every color to suit your mood or day of the week. A little divine intervention was sometimes needed for just the right choice. "I'm thinking Jesus would pick the red bracelet today and maybe the turquoise one tomorrow." Talk about a colorful way to proclaim your faith.

2. LOGO RIP-OFF SHIRT

Oh, snap! Your Looney Tunes shirts just weren't making the theological statement that you were going for? No problem! The Rodeo Drive of Christian fashion (aka the local Christian bookstore) had you covered. Using blatant plagiarism of nationally recognized company logos and slogans from Coca-Cola, Sprite, and 7UP, you could easily show everyone that you were: relevant enough to know soft-drink logos; a fan of bad puns; and in favor of whatever the opposite of creativity is. Cool beans! At only $9.97 per shirt, that's a value. Don't forget your Family Christian Stores Perk Card to help you earn that 25 percent coupon on your next logo rip-off shirt.

3. PURITY RING

If you were pumped after hearing "I Don't Want It," that meant you were ready for a legit purity ring. Are you saying that you don't want sex for now? Yep. Talk to the hand and peep this purity bling. This gold-plated heart with a cross on it told everyone everything they needed to know about your deeply personal, yet public, commitment to wait for your mate. If your ring coordinated with the ring of your crush, well, that's a sign from above that you were the next Out of the Grey. If your crush had silver, but you had gold, then it was common knowledge that it was best to keep him or her in the Friends (are Friends Forever) zone. Unfortunately, since you "kissed dating goodbye," you would never really know for sure.

Sometimes, your basic 90s Christian kid wardrobe needed a little something extra to truly make it 'da bomb, something that would shout to the world, "Don't Censor Me!" Maybe you were headed to a weekend youth retreat in Gatlinburg or better yet a church camp in

Panama City, Florida. It's time to up your game. Word. Here were the go-to items that could take your righteous style to the next level:

- **The Teen Study Bible (NIV).** The bold paint splatter design on the hard or soft cover complemented any logo rip-off shirt or your favorite artist's colorful vest. It's a must-have for See You at the Pole.
- **Favorite CCM artist shirt.** Sometimes the 90s logo rip-off shirts just weren't specific enough to display your keen and sophisticated musical tastes to the world around you. How is everyone going to know that you love "The Great Adventure" if you don't have a shirt of SCC on a horse? A "Jesus Freak" shirt was always a smart choice, no matter what the occasion. However, if you were lucky enough to have an "If you're happy and you know it, bang your head" Audio Adrenaline shirt, you were an absolute legend.
- **Baby-doll dress.** For that kinda girl who wanted to show off that purity ring, she would have chosen a baby-doll dress for the outfit of the day. If you were feeling as if it was a lovely day, you might choose an Out of Eden plaid print. If you were feeling as if the world was a lonely place, you might choose a Jaci Velasquez flower print. You'd be looking as pretty as a Kentucky rose. Whatever the outfit choice, your skirt was never too tight for a nice evening at the Olive Garden.

There you have it, the righteous style of the 90s Christian kid. Socially acceptable…at least back then.

LIZ HUMOR

©Liz King

"GOD"

(1996)

Songwriters: Rebecca St. James and Tedd T

Artist: Rebecca St. James

Album: *God*

Genesis 1:1-8–In the beginning, God created the heavens and the earth. The earth was without form and void, and darkness was over the face of the deep. And the Spirit of God was hovering over the face of the waters.

And God said, "Let there be light," and there was light. And God saw that the light was good. And God separated the light from the darkness. God called the light Day, and the darkness he called Night. And there was evening and there was morning, the first day.

And God said, "Let there be an expanse in the midst of the waters, and let it separate the waters from the waters." And God made the expanse and separated the waters that were under the expanse from the waters that were above the expanse.

And it was so. And God called the expanse Heaven. And there was evening and there was morning, the second day.

Genesis 1:26–Then God said, "Let us make man in our image, after our likeness. And let them have dominion over the fish of the sea and over the birds of the heavens and over the livestock and over all the earth and over every creeping thing that creeps on the earth.

Psalm 8:4–What is man that you are mindful of him, and the son of man that you care for him?

Ecclesiastes 3:11–He has made everything beautiful in its time. Also, he has put eternity into man's heart, yet so that he cannot find out what God has done from the beginning to the end.

Isaiah 55:9–For as the heavens are higher than the earth, so are my ways higher than your ways and my thoughts than your thoughts.

1 John 5:11-12–And this is the testimony, that God gave us eternal life, and this life is in his Son. Whoever has the Son has life; whoever does not have the Son of God does not have life.

90S IMPRESSION

At first glance, the song is simply about the reality that I must believe in God because He's God.

TODAY'S IMPRESSION

While the 90s impression is correct, the realities go beyond. God made everything, including humans. He spoke into being the world, which was formless and void. Our hearts are formless and void as well. Only God, our Creator, can bring life into empty hearts.

Ask a class of four-year-olds a Bible question. No matter the question, you'll likely get one of two answers from the students. Say it with me in a little kid's voice: "God" and "Jesus." Right? At first glance, Rebecca St. James' "God" seems simple and straightforward.

The song appears rudimentary until you start looking at the lyrics! In this theologically rich writing, an incredible gospel narrative exists. We are part of that story, and it all starts with God and ends with God.

"God" begins with the Genesis creation account. Before everything, there was God. Imagine a reality in which nothing else exists except for the Father, Son, and Holy Spirit—no other thought, color, cell, or ion. The creation narrative gives descriptions of the earth using words such as dark, barren, empty, chaotic, disorganized, lifeless, and uninhabitable. In the very truest sense, it was complete and total void.

It is from that state of absolute darkness and chaos that God would create order, light, and life. How did God create life from nothing? He spoke it.

Indulge me, if you will, and partake in a little experiment. It's safe to say that many of you reading this love chocolate. Open your mouth and utter the word "chocolate" and see if a blessing of sweet milky goodness appears.

How did you do? Outside of some Copperfield-esque illusion, you could not summon the power to make something appear by the power of your word. However, that is precisely how God created the world. Genesis 1:1 states, "In the beginning, God created the heavens and the earth." The Hebrew word for "created" is "bara," which literally means God spoke creation into existence. To help me remember this Hebrew term and idea, I often use a play on the word. Imagine God saying, "Alakazam…BARA!" That is essentially what God did.

From the void, by God's word alone, all life was created. We cannot comprehend it, yet being incomprehensible is what makes God's plan so beautifully divine. He is above us! The late R.C. Sproul contends, "God is self-existent and eternal in His being, and He alone has the ability to create things out of nothing." (*Everyone's a Theologian*, 91)

The song "God" then jumps from the creation narrative to us in the present. We each have a void inside that we seek to fill. How God fills the void on a universal scale can tell us a lot about how He fills the void in us on a very personal scale. He does it the very same way—through His Word.

Because of sin, our hearts are void—dark, barren, empty, chaotic, disorganized, lifeless, and uninhabitable. Nevertheless, we know the emptiness inside cannot be all there is (See Ecclesiastes 3:11; Romans 1:18-22.). In our attempt to fill our hearts with all kinds of stuff, we remain restless. A remedy for our condition exists: Jesus, the Living Word of God.

When John's Gospel states that "In the beginning was the Word, and the Word was with God, and the Word was God. He was in the beginning with God," it should knock the socks right out of our Birkenstocks (See John 1:1.). John understood that Jesus is the "Word of God" that creates life in us. He creates order out of chaos, light out of darkness, and fullness out of emptiness. Our physical and spiritual existence is made possible through God's Living Word—Jesus Christ.

In conjunction with the Hebrew term "bara," in which God speaks things into creation, is the Hebrew word "dabar." This particular Old Testament idea combines "word" and "deed." God speaks, and His word accomplishes a divine deed. In John 1, the Greek word used for "Word" is "logos." It means precisely the same thing! Jesus, God in flesh, is the Living Word! He is literally the word and deed of the Father, who now comes to bring light into a dark world and dead hearts (See John 1:4-14.).

Do you see it? The One who fills the universe with life is the only one who can create in us a full heart, alive unto God. Only Him. Where everything else fails, God remains. St. Augustine of Hippo famously stated in his *Confessions*, "You have made us for yourself, O Lord, and our hearts are restless until they rest in you." (1.1)

Those who know Jesus personally receive eternal and abundant life. The eternal life of Jesus now resides in hearts that were once formless and void. The Holy Spirit, existing and creating in the beginning, now speaks life into our empty souls. And, thus, our prayer: "May the God of hope fill you with all joy and peace in believing, so that by the power of the Holy Spirit you may abound in hope" (Romans 15:13).

The Living Word now lives in us! Only God, who speaks things into being out of nothing, can make something as fantastic as this possible. We exchange empty hearts for abundant lives.

Who can give us endless love and boundless grace? Only God. Don't try to explain it any other way. It's God.

-Ashley

REFERENCED VERSES

- Genesis 1:1-8, 26
- Psalm 8:4
- Ecclesiastes 3:11
- Isaiah 55:9
- John 1:1-14
- Romans 1:18-22; 15:13
- 1 John 5:11-12

FOR FURTHER STUDY

- *Confessions*, St. Augustine (*https://www.gutenberg.org/ebooks/3296*)
- *Everyone's a Theologian: An Introduction to Systematic Theology*, R.C. Sproul
- *Hymns of the Father: The Trinity Project Book 1*, Cameron Frank, Preston Norman, and Nathan Drake
- *The Case for the Creator: A Journalist Investigates Scientific Evidence That Points Toward God*, Lee Strobel
- *The Cross of Christ*, John Stott

"THE ROBE"

(1993)

Songwriter: Wes King

Artist: Wes King

Album: *The Robe*

Genesis 3:21–And the LORD God made for Adam and for his wife garments of skins and clothed them.

Job 29:14–I put on righteousness, and it clothed me; my justice was like a robe and a turban.

Isaiah 64:6–We have all become like one who is unclean, and all our righteous deeds are like a polluted garment. We all fade like a leaf, and our iniquities, like the wind, take us away."

Jeremiah 23:6b–And this is the name by which he will be called: 'The LORD is our righteousness.'

Galatians 3:27–For as many of you as were baptized into Christ have put on Christ.

90S IMPRESSION

Jesus gives us new righteous garments to wear when we accept Him as Lord and Savior. These garments mark us each as one of His and result from devotion to Jesus and being in a relationship with Him.

TODAY'S IMPRESSION

God demands complete and perfect holiness, and we are incapable of the righteousness needed to gird ourselves. In our sinful and weary state, we are utterly dependent on the righteousness of God, and our faith in Him grants a holy standing as He imputes His righteousness upon us.

Have you ever had *that* dream? You know the dream: the one that so many people embarrassingly admit. Maybe you are in class at school, in the grocery store, or at a sporting event, and naked as a jaybird. As another old-school musician, Ray Stevens, mused, you are only wearing a smile! Of course, you probably weren't smiling if you had that dream!

Thankfully, it is only a dream. You wake up, and the horror is over. But the reality of the situation in light of our sin is not a dream, and it is nothing to smile about.

The result of the fall of man and his sinful state is that every one of us is lost, broken, cold, and lonely. You could even say, naked. In our sin, embarrassment, and shame, we run to the dressing room of performance and do our best to try to put some clothes on. Yet, our fig leaves of effort never really cover us. The emptiness of a weary soul will never fill itself through self-pursuit.

Our only option is to depend on God's righteousness and put our hope in Him. He will fill us. Indeed, He will clothe us in His righteousness.

So, how does God clothe our nakedness, brokenness, and sinfulness with His righteousness?

In his 1993 hit, "The Robe," Wes King expounded upon this idea of how we come to God, what we bring to the table, and how we stand in our nakedness, utterly dependent on Christ's righteousness to clothe us.

Each of us are cold and lonely with empty hands worn by the toil of sin and life. Completely exhausted, we feel unworthy. Fear overcomes.

To sum it all up, we are lost and hopeless.

However, Jesus provides a way. Recognizing our current state is the right starting place. The song encourages us to come to Jesus just the way we are. And when we come, naked and ashamed, having faith in Christ, a covering awaits. We receive it by faith.

To get a complete picture, let's go to the fall in the garden of Eden and look at the original naked sinners, Adam and Eve.

In Genesis 3, the fall takes place, and we all know the story well. Yes, the serpent tempted the world's first couple as they did what God commanded them not to do. Upon their partaking of the fruit, they plunged into sin. Unfortunately, they took us with them.

Sin was birthed in them (and us), and they were ashamed and aware of their newfound "nakedness." What did they do? They sewed fig leaves and made themselves garments.

However, these garments were not suitable! I know how the Sunday School picture books portrayed the fig leaf speedo and ivy bikini, so we can only imagine. By His grace, God covered them. This act of God was a picture of the doctrine of grace that would continue to ring throughout Scripture and culminate in the life, death, and resurrection of Jesus Christ.

Consequently, because Adam and Eve's clothing wasn't suitable, in Genesis 3:21, God made them some new designer clothing out of animal skin. If you aren't looking, you might miss an important point here. For the first time in human history, something had to give up its life to cover sin. An animal was sacrificed, thus giving foresight into a coming sacrificial system and, eventually, the death of Christ. " For the wages of sin is death, but the free gift of God is eternal life in Christ Jesus our Lord" (Romans 6:23).

As we meditate on this idea, we must realize that we cannot suitably cover ourselves, and we rely on the life and death of Jesus to cover us.

In pursuit of heavenly and holy gain, humans pursue righteousness through various means of religion and morality. Even these well-intentioned efforts are only fig leaves, or as the prophet Isaiah stated in another way, "polluted rags."

Our only hope is outside of ourselves. We must, by faith, be clothed in the righteousness of Jesus.

Theologians call this imputed righteousness. R.C. Sproul explained the giant theological idea in layman's terms: "As soon as people take hold of Christ by faith, the merit of Christ is transferred to them." (*Everyone's a Theologian*, 235) Essentially, when we trust in Jesus, and He saves us, we are credited with His righteousness. He lived perfectly and, indeed, was the ultimate sacrifice. We have faith in Jesus' righteous life and death and are justified by faith alone in Christ.

In his book, *Faith Alone: The Doctrine of Justification*, Thomas Schreiner explained the parallel between Adam and Jesus, given by Paul in Romans 5:12-19. We inherited sin through Adam. "Conversely, Jesus, in contrast to Adam, was the obedient one, and hence life and righteousness comes through him." (184)

Essentially, we all either belong to Adam or Christ. And Adam's fig leaves don't actually cover up our sin and nakedness! We need the perfect covering that comes from the Son of God, who exchanges our fig leaves and even our exhausted efforts of self-righteousness and sacrifice for a robe of righteousness.

Think about it. A holy and just God demands our righteousness. God calls us to adhere to everything in the law, and if we do not, Paul said we are cursed (See Galatians 3:10.). Jesus alone did keep God's law perfectly (See Hebrews 4:15.), and "For our sake he made him to be sin who knew no sin, so that in him we might become the righteousness of God" (2 Corinthians 5:21).

What God requires, Christ provides. By faith in Him, He places a robe of righteousness on us.

A famous sermon by Charles Spurgeon, "The Lord Our Righteousness," inspired Wes King's penning of this song. In the sermon, Spurgeon discussed Jeremiah 23:6, which states, "And this is the name by which he will be called: The LORD is our righteousness."

Spurgeon got to the heart of the matter by drilling home the notion that God cannot pardon a man because of righteous efforts. Spurgeon mused, "Surely, my Brethren, none of you are so drunk as to think that this righteousness can be worked out by yourselves." To be wholly clothed in the death and life of Christ is our only hope.

We can never perfectly keep the law, so that can't cover us. We can never be good enough, so that can't cover us. To be sure, fig leaves don't work either. Even the animal skins were a picture of something that would one day be permanent. We can only be pardoned and seen as righteous in the eyes of God by the covering of Christ.

So what are we to do? We come just as we are, and put our trust in Christ alone.

- Ashley

REFERENCED VERSES

- Genesis 3:21
- Job 29:14
- Isaiah 63:6
- Jeremiah 23:6
- Romans 3:23; 5:12-19
- 2 Corinthians 5:21
- Galatians 3:10, 27
- Hebrews 4:15

FOR FURTHER STUDY

- *Everyone's a Theologian: An Introduction to Systematic Theology,* R.C. Sproul
- *Faith Alone–The Doctrine of Justification: What the Reformers Taught…and Why It Still Matters,* Thomas R. Schreiner
- "The Lord Our Righteousness," Charles Spurgeon (*https://www.spurgeon.org/resource-library/sermons/jehovah-tsidkenu-the-lord-our-righteousness/#flipbook/*)
- *The Naked Gospel: The Truth You May Never Hear In Church,* Andrew Farley

"STOMP"

(1997)

Songwriters: George Clinton, Jr., Kirk Franklin, Garry Shider, Walter Morrison

Artist: Kirk Franklin (featuring Cheryl James)

Album: *God's Property from Kirk Franklin's Nu Nation*

> **Romans 8:31-39**–What then shall we say to these things? If God is for us, who can be against us? He who did not spare his own Son but gave him up for us all, how will he not also with him graciously give us all things? Who shall bring any charge against God's elect? It is God who justifies. Who is to condemn? Christ Jesus is the one who died—more than that, who was raised—who is at the right hand of God, who indeed is inter-ceding for us. Who shall separate us from the love of Christ? Shall tribulation, or distress, or persecution, or famine, or nakedness, or danger, or sword? As it is written, "For your sake we are being killed all the day long; we are regarded as sheep to be slaughtered."
>
> No, in all these things we are more than conquerors through him who loved us. For I am sure that neither death nor life, nor

angels nor rulers, nor things present nor things to come, nor powers, nor height nor depth, nor anything else in all creation, will be able to separate us from the love of God in Christ Jesus our Lord.

90S IMPRESSION

When I think and sing about Jesus, it ushers me into an emotionally charged state. In fact, I want to dance, clap, and stomp!

TODAY'S IMPRESSION

Although positive emotions are not bad things, singing and thinking about Jesus is so much more than a spiritual pep rally. The true reality of what Christ has done makes me more than a conqueror. Life will be hard at times. Even so, in Christ, I am an overcomer.

The first time I heard Kirk Franklin's gospel throwdown "Stomp," I was a student pastor in seminary, and our youth group learned to perform it in a puppet show. Nothing says 90s ministry and music like puppet ministry! The puppets were all shapes and sizes–giant heads, odd noses, frogs and birds alike, collectively rapping like MC Hammer and singing soulfully. Those puppets were having church, I tell ya! Of course, through all the dancing, bobbing heads, and syncopated lines, they all came together perfectly at what part? You guessed it. "STOMP!"

You could not help but feel something down deep in your bones! Was this song about dancing? You dance and get excited when you hear it, right?

However, a tremendously biblical idea beyond the energy exists in this head-bopping praise anthem. How do we as Christians find victory throughout the many struggles of life? In Christ Jesus, we move beyond the normal victimized mentality of one defeated and become conquerors!

The text from Romans 8 sets the stage perfectly: "If God is for us, who can be against us?" No foe exists that can defeat one of God's elect.

It seems the influx of superhero movies in recent years is at an all-time high. We love a protagonist who can stomp out evil and who stands for good, suspending reality for us (if only for two hours) as we embark on the adventures of these fictitious characters. From Batman to Iron Man, Avengers to X-Men, these heroes rule the silver screen. We like a hero. We like a conqueror. We like "Super."

Away from the movie screen and into real life, challenges mount and life seeks to swallow us up. Kirk Franklin got straight to the point as he talked about life's struggles and circumstances that were getting him down. In recent years, Franklin has been candid about his own personal hardships. Franklin grew up fatherless. He has struggled with anxiety and depression, overcame a porn addiction, and at the age of 15 admits to helping pay for his girlfriend's abortion. Being in the lime-light brings its own challenges. You never know what someone is going through. These lyrics are not mere pen on paper, but real-life struggles.

The apostle Paul asserted exactly what some of those struggles are. The list includes metaphors and harsh realities: tribulation, distress, perse-cution, famine, nakedness, danger, and sword. In fact, "We are being killed all the day long as we are regarded as sheep to be slaughtered" (See Romans 8:36.).

Thankfully, there is something else that is "Super," and more mind-blowing than any comic-book hero. A relationship with the living God through His Son, Jesus Christ, transforms us! If you have by faith trusted in the blood and resurrection of Jesus and know Him person-ally, you, my friend, are a super conqueror!

"No, in all these things we are more than conquerors through him that loved us" (verse 37). This pain-stomping verse proclaims something remarkably splendid for God's children. It would have been enough for Paul to state that we are "conquerors" in Christ Jesus. However, he wanted to drive his point home and take it to another level.

Greek scholar Rick Renner unveiled some "sparkling gems" about the biblical idea of "more than a conqueror." The phrase "more than conquerors" comes from the Greek word *hupernikos*, a compound of the words *huper* and *nikos*. By bringing the words together, Paul made an incredible decree in one amazing statement about those who are in Christ. The words "more than" comes from the Greek word *huper*, meaning *over, above, and beyond*. It carries with it the idea of superiority and unmatched, unsurpassed power. (*Sparkling Gems from the Greek*, 37-38)

Then there is the word for conquerors, *nikos*. It details an overcomer, champion, victor, or master. A *nikos* is a force to be reckoned with. The word *nikos* wasn't enough to stand on its own to prove Paul's point, so he combined the words to prove his point.

When you put the words together, they declare that in Jesus Christ you are *an overwhelming conqueror, a paramount victor*! We could interpret it as a gigantic, dynamic, overwhelming, phenomenal, conquering force! (Renner, 37-38) Superman doesn't hold a candle to the power we have in Christ!

We are super conquerors!

Coming from a broken home and dealing with some huge challenges in my own life at a very early age, I learned to embrace the truth of who lived in me. Amid life's challenges, I would not be a victim. People experience gut-wrenching unexplainable tragedies. Homes fall apart like sand castles. Temptation and trials knock on everyone's door. Still, no matter what comes our way, we are more than conquerors through Him who loves us.

Believers in danger of death and persecution all across the globe live out this verse daily. They reside in China, the Middle East, and Africa. As culture and spiritual landscapes change, the affliction could be coming soon to a neighborhood near you. Should this cause us to give up? Will we quit? Is "victim" our identity?

Absolutely not! The apostle Paul was clear that nothing can separate from what we have in Jesus. The miracle of this union is not something we ever achieve but receive. And by grace, we proclaim it!

A great deal of these thoughts may seem illogical. Dietrich Bonhoeffer, discussing discipleship and the cross, quotes Martin Luther, stating, "Bewilderment is the true comprehension." (*The Cost of Discipleship*, 93) This mysterious reality is incredibly comforting. The super ability I possess to overcome is not me, nor from me. I love how Mark Batterson sought to grasp divine power in *In a Pit With a Lion on a Snowy Day*: "You have to start by trying to comprehend the infiniteness of God so that you can believe He can help you to defy the odds." (168)

If you are a Christian, take hold of the God who has taken hold of you (See Philippians 3:12-14.)! If you are struggling, find peace in an intimate union with Jesus. No matter what kind of "stuff" you are going through, trust that you are more than a conqueror in Christ Jesus. Kind of makes you want to . . . well, you know the song.

Side note: This is not prosperity gospel. Life is hard. Sin, struggle, and afflictions are real. The Bible never promises that living life and being a Christian will be easy. But what we know for sure is that when our Hope is in Christ, and we are living in that Hope, we have everything we need to overcome! Hope in Jesus Christ does not disappoint. Rest in Him. You are a super conqueror!

- Ashley

REFERENCED VERSES

- Romans 8:31-39
- Philippians 3:12-14

FOR FURTHER STUDY

- *Church Boy: My Music & My Life*, Kirk Franklin

- *In a Pit With a Lion on a Snowy Day: How to Survive and Thrive When Opportunity Roars*, Mark Batterson
- *Sparkling Gems from the Greek*, Rick Renner
- *The Cost of Discipleship*, Dietrich Bonhoeffer
- *To Live is Christ to Die is Gain*, Matt Chandler, Jared C. Wilson

"CRUCIFIED WITH CHRIST"
(1995)

Songwriters: David Allen Clark, Donald A. Koch, Denise Phillips, and Randy Phillips

Artist: Phillips, Craig, & Dean

Album: *Trust*

> **Galatians 2:20**–I have been crucified with Christ. It is no longer I who live, but Christ who lives in me. And the life I now live in the flesh I live by faith in the Son of God, who loved me and gave himself for me.

90S IMPRESSION

As a born again Christian, my identity is in how much I can impress God and others as I muster up the inner-strength to do both.

TODAY'S IMPRESSION

The old me no longer exists. At salvation, Jesus becomes my life, and from there, I live. He is my identity.

No need to brush off those VHS tapes and watch *Unsolved Mystery* reruns in an attempt to discover deep meaning in the Phillips, Craig, and Dean 90s classic "Crucified with Christ." The trio's powerful anthem proclaims biblical truth straight from pages of Scripture. Life-changing realities of Galatians 2:20 set the timbre, and the glorious declaration from Paul can be misunderstood and rarely talked about.

Here is the oft-missed meaning: If you are a Christian, they crucified you when they crucified Jesus.

I once heard it said that Galatians 2:20 was the "Christian's John 3:16." The more I explore the great mystery of Paul being crucified with Christ, I tend to agree. If John 3:16 gives a great summation for understanding a proper soteriology for the lost, then Galatians 2:20 contains a lifelong lesson to understand and live by after salvation.

What does "crucified with Christ" actually mean? Is it the whole "take up my cross daily" idea? As we seek to answer what Paul implied, the reality is that Christians rarely express to others, "I am crucified."

We often say, "Jesus died for my sins." "He died for me." "Jesus was crucified and rose again." Or even, "As I put my trust in His death and resurrection, I find salvation and enter into a relationship with Him." Now those statements undoubtedly assert biblical truth. However, it is rare to hear someone say, "I am crucified."

Hmmmmm. Very interesting. Yet, look at the text! That is precisely what Paul declared. Was he saying we are dead as humans or snuffed out of existence and no longer exist? In a previous devotion, we learned that being in Christ provides a new way to be human. To be sure, our humanity is still here, but we operate differently. We are new creations. God makes us "alive in Christ." Herein lies the beauty of understanding Paul's remarkable words.

As Christians, we now *live* by faith in Christ. And yes, the old you and I are dead. We indeed give our lives to Christ. Our old lives, that is. Moreover, when we gave God our old lives, He killed them.

Newsflash!: The old you no longer exists! A heart transplant has taken place. You could almost think of it as if God swapped your old DNA for new DNA, spiritually speaking. How amazing is that? Lest we forget 2 Corinthians 5:17, that we are in Christ, and are new creations. "The old has passed away; behold, the new has come."

I used to think that this idea of being crucified with Christ is something I did. Perhaps it was something I had to do—as if I could bring sacrifices to God, and He might stamp His approval on my amazing sacrifices and performance and save me. In reality, the verse teaches that when Jesus died on the cross, by faith in Him, I was there also. I am co-crucified with Christ.

How is this possible? If one digs a bit deeper, Paul's precise wording explains.

The word *crucified* derives from a compound word, containing *with* and *crucified*. When they crucified Christ on the cross, God crucified Paul as well. What occurred to Christ physically took place for Paul legally and spiritually. I use the term "co-crucified," as that is what Paul wrote, and by Paul's faith, that is what took place. By faith, we were there too. You and I get the same results Paul did; Jesus becomes our life!

The reality of Jesus becoming our life is possible because Paul himself participated in the crucifixion. The cross is where he found forgiveness and life. As humans born depraved who inherit Adam's sin, we each seek an escape from the penalty we deserve, which is death. When we are co-crucified, just as we have been crucified with Christ, we can now enter into a life-giving relationship with Christ.

Even more, the tense of the verb "have been crucified" means that Paul's crucifixion had a permanent effect. Think about it. One cannot *kind of* be crucified. A crucifixion is as bloody, severe, and permanent as it gets. Furthermore, the apostle Paul's crucifixion was not something that he did but had been done to him by trusting in God. It took place by faith for each of us at Calvary! God crucified Paul on the cross, and he stood as one crucified when he wrote this letter. His crucifixion, as well as ours, has finished results in the present.

Our very identity is now with Christ forever! Yes, we have been crucified. Nevertheless, Paul asserts that he lives! We are born again with new lives. By faith in Jesus, we experience a spiritual crucifixion. Jesus rose from the dead, and we did too! Remembering Jesus is our very life is the heart of how we function.

What about the teaching of denying ourselves? Aren't we told to take up our cross and follow Jesus? Do we die daily to ourselves? Think of it this way: Jesus took up His cross and went to Calvary, and that is where we must go as well! God doesn't tell us to commit spiritual suicide. If we correctly understand Galatians 2:20, we are already dead! We follow Jesus to His death, resulting in us being raised with Him, alive, through His resurrection.

Denying yourself daily is remembering you are dead!

I have often heard that the cross is an instrument of death, and we must crucify ourselves. Have you ever stopped to realize the method of death of that of the cross? They kill you! You cannot hang yourself on a cross. The type of death entailed in crucifixion is one performed on you. Often, when I deal with daily struggles as I follow Jesus, I deny flesh, and remember I am already dead!

As I do that, I proclaim that Jesus is my very life! Jesus paid the ultimate price so you could have a new identity in Him and a new life in Him. Live, breathe, and walk in Him. He is your life!

How do we access this new life and enter into this co-crucifixion? Paul gave us the answer. "The life I now live in the flesh I live by faith in the Son of God, who loved me and gave himself for me" (Galatians 2:20). It is by faith. To be sure, faith is not just guessing and hoping. According to Hebrews 11:1, faith is the assurance, or the "substance" as the KJV states, of things hoped for, the conviction of things not seen. Did you catch it? Faith. Is. Substance. Yes, substance. Let that sink in.

Through faith, we are born again into a living hope through His resurrection (See 1 Peter 1:3.)! You cannot get more substance than the Son of God, alive.

Phillips, Craig, and Dean remind us that it is by His strength. Hallelujah! I am crucified with Christ, but in Jesus, I live!

- Ashley

REFERENCED VERSES

- Matthew 16:24
- Luke 9:23
- Romans 5:8-9; 6:23
- 1 Corinthians 15:21
- 2 Corinthians 5:17
- Galatians 2:19-20
- Ephesians 2:5
- 1 Peter 1:3

FOR FURTHER STUDY

- *Identity: Who You Are in Christ*, Eric Geiger
- *The Cross of Christ*, John Stott
- *The Naked Gospel: The Truth That You May Never Hear in Church*, Andrew Farley

YOU'LL ALWAYS REMEMBER YOUR FIRSTS

BY KEVIN MCNEESE, PRESIDENT AND FOUNDER OF
NEWRELEASETODAY.COM

My wife and I were typical new parents. Our journals and cameras documented every single first in our daughter's life. Her first smile. Her first step. Her first word. Fast forward 16 years as we navigate our mid-40s, and we're still doing it, albeit with less exuberance and celebration. First dates and first cars are some of the last steps toward adulthood, which means those firsts are starting to hurt a bit more as our little girl grows up.

Without sounding crass, it's true what they say: "You always remember your firsts." They are monumental moments in time followed by a thousand less significant moments repeating the same thing–which is why I'll never forget my first Christian music festival and first Christian artist crush.

I was 15 years old, fresh from the experience of discovering an entire world of Christian music that was radically transforming my life. A few years earlier, a friend put on a cassette tape of Audio Adrenaline's *Don't Censor Me* (1993), a band I had never heard of. By the end of the third track, "Soulmate," I was absolutely hooked. This wasn't my mom's Amy Grant. Instead, the music was vibrant, energetic, and had some attitude and edge. From there, a barrage of Christian music flooded my ears at every waking moment from dozens of artists and bands such as Newsboys, Plankeye, Jars of Clay, Carman, dc Talk—and Rebecca St. James.

Christian music was breaking away from its contemporary roots, and I was growing up in the middle of it.

Part of that explosive expansion was the Christian music festival—an annual multi-night summer gathering of tens of thousands of Christian music fans camping on-site and absorbing multiple stages of genres of music rooted in faith. As someone who lived in the Northwest, music festivals were few and far between, but the major annual gathering at the time was Jesus Northwest '93 in Washington state. (Jesus Northwest was later rebranded Creation West and folded in 2017.)

I remember very little from this experience. Like any event where you're 30 years removed from its occurrence, details feel vague and foggy, but two moments are etched forever in my brain.

The first moment was waiting 45 minutes in a signing line for Church of Rhythm, a mid-90s band with a short two-album run. (It was produced by Max Hsu, who still works in the industry as a producer and photographer.) Their 1995 debut album resonated with urban beats, rap interludes, and many drums and bass. I loved it. Their second album, showcased during the Jesus Northwest tour, departed from their previous style and embraced more of a grunge/rock sound, leaving me a disgruntled fan.

When it was my turn in line, I looked the lead singer straight in the eyes instead of getting a signature and told him he had ruined an amazing band. I was such a punk. Even though their sophomore album, *Not Perfect*, became much adored and still holds up today in my opinion, (that title track is perfection), they disbanded shortly after.

The second memorable moment at Jesus Northwest happened in slow motion, and I can see it replay in my head like it was yesterday.

It was in the middle of the day, and I was rounding the corner to the main stage while the announcer introduced another new singer (almost all Christian music was new then). I froze while this 16-year-old woman came out on stage and began to belt out her hit debut single, "Here I Am." And there I was. Just her and me, and a few thousand other loser nobodies, enjoying a moment together. Destiny had arrived.

Rebecca St. James and I grew up together. We were similar ages, and loved Jesus and Christian music. Knowing each other's existence was the only missing ingredient needed to build a successful life together. That small factor never materialized, and looking back, I wonder what would have happened had my boldness to tell off a professional rock band would have carried over to her autograph line on that day at Jesus Northwest. I never dared to find out, but it probably would have been a hilarious ending to my first Christian artist crush at my first Christian music festival.

"NO CONDEMNATION"

(1994)

Songwriter: Chris Eaton

Artist: Lisa Bevill

Album: *All Because of You*

> **Romans 5:18**–Therefore, as one trespass led to condemnation for all men, so one act of righteousness leads to justification and life for all men.

> **Romans 8:1**–There is therefore now no condemnation for those who are in Christ Jesus.

90S IMPRESSION

There is no condemnation for those who trust in Jesus.

TODAY'S IMPRESSION

There is no condemnation for those who trust in Jesus because Jesus took on the penalty of my sin and justified me.

Homegirl Lisa B has one beautiful voice. In addition to her CCM career, she is the voice talent behind the famous Wrigley's Doublemint Gum jingle, as well as Stanley Steemer, Diet 7UP, and numerous other well-known national campaigns. She can make deep cleaning your carpets whilst chewing gum and drinking lemon and lime soda sound awesome.

Back in the 90s, when I was a teen, I once spotted her coming out of a Nashville restaurant, and I immediately accosted her in the parking lot for a picture. I still have it. She was so incredibly kind. In 2001, I watched her perform in Manhattan. After the show, I asked her to record the answering-machine greeting for our dorm room, and she did! Once again, she was incredibly gracious and patient. Lisa Bevill told our incoming callers, which were very few, to leave a message after the beep. I realize now the monetary value of the voice talent I asked to receive for free. Where was my chaperone that day? I'm still so incredibly mortified that I did that, but would I do it again? Heck, yes.

In a single song, Lisa can soothe with gentle tenderness and inspire with powerhouse conviction. You feel all the feels in "No Condemnation." Produced by Charlie Peacock and written by Chris Eaton, this song features her incredible ability to move the audience with emotion. I knew this song had to be in this book.

Lisa has mentioned that she loves that this song comes straight from Scripture, Romans 8:1– "There is therefore now no condemnation for those who are in Christ Jesus." These are words from Paul to the Roman Church, a mix of Gentiles and Jews. Through this letter, Paul worked through the themes of salvation and righteousness.

Paul used the term *condemnation*. This Greek word, *katakrima*, also means "penalty." Paul utilized a courtroom motif to speak of our standing before a holy and just Judge. Imagine yourself on trial in the cosmic courtroom now. The charges? You have sinned against God (See Romans 3:23.). Your penalty? The death sentence (See Romans 6:23.).

As the trial begins, accuser after accuser ascends to the witness stand. With a finger pointed squarely at you, each one names you as the culprit, the criminal. The evidence is stacked up against you. Not one receipt, incriminating photo, or witness is left unexamined. Your offenses against the righteous law of God are many. You, my friend, are a serial sinner. Was there even a single day that you didn't transgress? No. Even the sins you thought were hidden away out of sight, are revealed as key evidence. Your day in court has arrived, and it's not looking good for you.

Your defense? None.

The verdict is in. You rise to stand. Condemned or vindicated? Life or death?

Your case seems cut and dry. But, despite all the odds, you have a reason to hope–Jesus. You look to Him. He sees you. You put all your hope and faith in Him to save you. And, although you do not deserve it, He does save you just as He promised. He takes your place in front of the Judge and accepts the death sentence that was meant for you. Free from condemnation, you make it out of the courtroom alive. Not only that, the Judge declares you righteous, and your records have been wiped clean.

What an incredible turn of events! What has happened to make this possible? Reformationist Martin Luther referred to this as the "wonderful exchange," or sometimes called the "great exchange," whereby Jesus takes our sin and guilt upon Himself and places upon, or imputes, to us His righteousness. This is the Christian doctrine of justification. Luther explained,

> "That is the mystery which is rich in divine grace to sinners: wherein by a wonderful exchange our sins are no longer ours but Christ's and the righteousness of Christ not Christ's but

ours. He has emptied Himself of His righteousness that He might clothe us with it, and fill us with it.

And He has taken our evils upon Himself that He might deliver us from them... in the same manner as He grieved and suffered in our sins, and was confounded, in the same manner we rejoice and glory in His righteousness." (*Werke* 5: 608)

A wonderful exchange indeed. Dr. Ashley likes to explain justification as "just-as-if-I'd" never sinned–justified. Our justification is based on what Jesus Christ accomplished once and for all on the cross (See Romans 5:18.). As a gift to us, Jesus set us free from the penalty of our sin, satisfied the justice of God, and diverted the divine wrath of God. Christ's resurrection demonstrated that the wonderful exchange was successful (See Romans 4:25.)!

At the wonderful exchange, we see a Savior on the cross. All the lust in the world was there. Broken promises were there. Murder, killing, yes, hatred, and racism were there. Adultery, every form of abuse, all the pornography, all the drunkenness, all the perversion, greed, crime, idolatry–all of it was there. Not one single sin was held back from Him. All of it was laid upon Jesus when He hung on the cross.

At the climax of His sufferings, He cried out, "My God, My God, why have you forsaken me?" (Matthew 27:46). Those mysterious words mean that in that terrible moment, Jesus felt the unfathomable separation from God that was caused by our sin. This was the cost of our salvation.

Thank you, Jesus, our sunshine and joy, for your undying love. You have set us free. It's all because of You. To God alone be the glory! For those in Christ, there is now no condemnation.

- Rachel

REFERENCED VERSES

- Matthew 27:46
- Romans 3:23; 4:25; 6:23; 5:18; 8:1

FOR FURTHER STUDY

- *Jesus' Blood and Righteousness: Paul's Theology of Imputation,* Brian Vickers
- *The Cross of Christ,* John Stott

"IN CHRIST ALONE"

(1991)

Songwriters: Don Koch and Shawn Craig

Artist: Michael English

Album: *Michael English*

> **2 Corinthians 12:9**–But he said to me, "My grace is sufficient for you, for my power is made perfect in weakness." Therefore I will boast all the more gladly of my weaknesses, so that the power of Christ may rest upon me.

> **Galatians 6:14**–But far be it from me to boast except in the cross of our Lord Jesus Christ, by which the world has been crucified to me, and I to the world.

> **Ephesians 2:8-9**–For by grace you have been saved through faith. And this is not your own doing; it is the gift of God, not a result of works, so that no one may boast.

> **Ephesians 3:20-21**–Now to him who is able to do far more abundantly than all that we ask or think, according to the power at

work within us, to him be glory in the church and in Christ Jesus throughout all generations, forever and ever. Amen.

Philippians 3:9–And be found in him, not having a righteousness of my own that comes from the law, but that which comes through faith in Christ, the righteousness from God that depends on faith.

90S IMPRESSION

I must put my trust in Jesus as I navigate life.

TODAY'S IMPRESSION

God's grace is my only hope for eternity and Christian living. Anything I do or can do is only because of Jesus. And because of this, He alone receives praise and glory for all I do and for who I am.

My high school band director used to say after a good rehearsal, marching show, or concert, "Pat yourself on the back, but don't break your arm doing it." I don't know anyone who has ever broken their own arm patting themselves on the back, but if possible, we would. Isn't that what humans do? We love to pat ourselves on the back. We like credit. Most people love to get petted on like a golden retriever and get the itch of their egos scratched.

When it comes to our salvation, we deserve no pats or pets because we can't rebirth ourselves. Even the ability to live the Christian life has nothing to do with our performance level but our utter dependence on the strength and grace of God.

In Michael English's song "In Christ Alone" (not to be confused with the amazing modern worship hymn by Keith and Kristyn Getty), the writers get straight to the heart of our faith and who it is that gets the credit for the spiritual victories in our lives. Much like the Getty's mega worship hit, this oozes with Christology and Soteriology.

Honestly, "In Christ Alone" is one of the most theologically rich CCM songs of the 90s. If you are a student of theology, you have learned about the five *solas* (Latin for "alone") of the Protestant Reformation. The five *solas* state that Christians are saved by grace alone (See Romans 3:10-12; Ephesians 2:8-9.), through faith alone (See Romans 4:4-5; 5:5-8.), in Christ alone (See John 14:6; Acts 4:12; Romans 10:9.), as revealed by Scripture alone (See 2 Timothy 3:16-17; 2 Peter 1:21.), to the glory of God alone (See John 6:44; Titus 3:4-5.).

"In Christ Alone" focuses primarily on the third *sola*, that we are saved by Christ alone. However, all of the principles flow freely in that divine truth.

As humans, we tend to link our identity to our performance. Maybe when you were growing up, you were a Bible Drill champion. Perhaps you never won at Bible Drill, but you excelled in sports or music. Or maybe you just enjoyed victory in crazy youth group games or a rousing game of wallyball at a youth lock-in.

But do those victories and accomplishments bring about anything that lasts? It becomes routine to live life-chasing victories. Eventually, we see life as chasing after whatever victory we can accomplish, and it is easy for that "chasing" to become our identity. And therein lies the key to the entire idea. What brings you the most satisfaction, and where is your trust? It must be in Christ alone!

The writer of Hebrews reminded us,

> Now may the God of peace who brought again from the dead our Lord Jesus, the great shepherd of the sheep, by the blood of the eternal covenant, equip you with everything good that you may do his will, working in us that which is pleasing in his sight, through Jesus Christ, to whom be glory forever and ever. Amen (13:20-21).

God, the "Great Equipper," gives us everything we need.

If we want to get down to the nitty-gritty, an interesting question is this: Why is trusting in Jesus the only possibility of salvation in Heaven? Or, from a comparative world religion and apologetics stand-point, what makes Christianity any different than all the other religions of the world?

I have asked that question many times throughout my studies, and I believe the answer awakens us to the reality of grace. The saving truth of the gospel message will become evident if we compare Christianity with other possible ways to get to Heaven or other various paths to God. Non-Christian methods base salvation on our climbing the ladder to get to God (or Heaven, nirvana, and so forth). The ladder will be one of good works, religion, church, morals, and so forth. However, if we understand that we can never be good enough to get to God, we see that the ladder we try to climb will never enable us to get there. And that is precisely why Jesus came! Instead of our trying to reach Him, He came down to us!

In John 14:6, Jesus states, "I am the way, and the truth, and the life. No one comes to the Father except through me." Jesus came down to Earth and lived the life we could not live. Then He died the death we all deserve as a perfect righteous sacrifice and substitute. Jesus came down and made what was impossible for us possible. Our job? Have faith in Him.

In Christ Alone!

We cannot save ourselves, and Paul was clear that salvation is by grace through faith in Christ. It is the gift of God, and we can't take any of the credit! The song reminds us that we must guard against pride and success. We can have all the trophies in the world, but they will never equal the grace of God in which we stand. We rest in Jesus. We learn to walk in Jesus. And yes, we stand in Jesus!

In his encouraging exposition of Ephesians, *Sit, Walk, Stand,* Watchman Nee reminded us of these truths:

"Only those who sit can stand. Our power for standing, as for walking, lies in our having first been made to sit together with

Christ. The Christian's walk and warfare alike derive their strength from his position there. If he is not sitting before God he cannot hope to stand before the enemy." (56)

In Christ alone, we trust and find the reality of life lived through the power of the cross. This power appeased God's wrath and served as our ransom. Christ alone grants us power over the devil and the power of our flesh. Christ alone cancels our debt and forgives our sins. We are no longer condemned, live loved, and God makes us saints. And this is all by the power of God so that He can receive the glory for it all!

It all makes me want to get out of the way, quit trying so hard, and put my trust in the only place that matters: Christ alone. These glorious facts remind me of my true reward and satisfaction. My identity is not in what I do or accomplish but in who I trust. As we continue to learn in these devotions, Jesus is my life. He is my salvation and my hope. Jesus alone.

-Ashley

REFERENCED VERSES

- Mark 10:45
- John 14:6
- Romans 3:25; 8:3
- 2 Corinthians 12:9
- Galatians 3:13; 6:14
- Ephesians 2:8-9; 3:20-21; 5:2
- Philippians 3:9
- Colossians 2:13
- Hebrews 10:14; 13:20-21
- 1 John 4:10

FOR FURTHER STUDY

- *Sit, Walk, Stand: The Process of Christian Maturity,* Watchman Nee
- *The Passion of Jesus Christ: Fifty Reasons Why He Came to Die,* John Piper
- *The Pleasures of God: Meditations on God's Delight in Being God,* John Piper

"THE GREAT ADVENTURE"

(1992)

Songwriters: Steven Curtis Chapman and Geoff Moore

Artist: Steven Curtis Chapman

Album: *The Great Adventure*

1 Corinthians 2:9–But, as it is written, "What no eye has seen, nor ear heard, nor the heart of man imagined, what God has prepared for those who love him."

Ephesians 2:4-10–But God, being rich in mercy, because of the great love with which he loved us, even when we were dead in our trespasses, made us alive together with Christ—by grace you have been saved— and raised us up with him and seated us with him in the heavenly places in Christ Jesus, so that in the coming ages he might show the immeasurable riches of his grace in kindness toward us in Christ Jesus. For by grace you have been saved through faith. And this is not your own doing; it is the gift of God, not a result of works, so that no one may boast. For we are his workmanship, created in Christ Jesus for good works, which God prepared beforehand, that we should walk in them.

90S IMPRESSION

Being a Christian is a fantastic journey, and we need to get on our horses and get going!

TODAY'S IMPRESSION

The amazing adventure of the Christian life is living in God's amazing grace.

Saddle Up! Are there any more fitting words to begin talking about Steven Curtis Chapman's iconic song, "The Great Adventure"? I know what many of you are doing. You are reminiscing about the video and picturing SCC at the ranch or on his motorcycle. Something about that opening guitar riff gets the 90s CCM juices flowing like none other. As nostalgic as that is for me, the song's message rings true now more than ever.

As I have grown in my understanding of grace over the years, my understanding of these lyrics has deepened. I grew up in a "religious" home. Although I am thankful that I was raised in church and came to follow Jesus at an early age, I don't know if I ever understood grace.

I sang about "Amazing Grace," but never grasped it. I knew that Jesus saved me from my sin, but it took years for the light bulb of grace to go off in my head. From my perspective, my religion depended on my performance more than God's grace.

When I began to see grace–that I was utterly dependent on God for all of my life and my salvation–it made me love Jesus more. The walls of legalistic, long-faced religion began to crack and fall around me. His love struck me like a lightning bolt.

Clouds of dust rolled back and I began to see the frontier of God's amazing grace before me. Do you see it too? I believe that we quickly forget the overwhelming goodness of the gospel. As we think about the grace of God and Jesus' glorious gospel, a good question to ponder is: *What makes grace so amazing?*

SCC is known for depth in his music; I see it in "The Great Adventure." One thing I always appreciated about SCC was the Scripture that he included within the liner notes of his CDs and, yes, cassette tapes. There was something special about opening the liner notes and reading the Bible verses he paired with each song.

For "The Great Adventure," the liner notes tell us to look at 1 Corinthians 2:9 and Ephesians 2:4-10. These passages are a great place to start understanding the vast expanse of God's grace and what this great adventure is all about.

In Corinthians, Paul hit on a great Christian truth that we should never underestimate: What God prepares for us is so much more than we can ever imagine. Or, to quote another SCC song, there is "More to This Life!" Grace is amazing, because it goes beyond what we can imagine. God does things for us that rise above any human high! When we get an abundant life in Jesus, God's grace comes in and gives an abundance of love, forgiveness, security, and purpose. God does more than save us by grace. He completely transforms our lives by His grace!

The great adventure of the Christian life won't be going through the motions of staunch religion. Jesus came to stop all that! The great adventure will be holding on to Jesus and seeing where He will take you! It will involve living out your faith and growing. There will be mountains, and yes, valleys.

In *The Rest of the Gospel,* Dan Stone and David Gregory explained how many Christians see Christianity. People get saved and forgiven, and then one day, go to Heaven. Do you see the gaping hole? What about the "in-between?" The time between salvation and Heaven becomes defined by survival. For many, it's not a good adventure. Life becomes an adventure that we prefer to bypass. "That's good news! It's not religion. It's not us doing something to earn God's approval. It's He giving us Himself. It's 'Christ in you, the hope of glory.'" (251) Christ in me makes the "in-between" a great adventure because I live life in Him and His amazing grace.

Things often defined as "religious" will undoubtedly be a part of where God leads. Yet the motivation is different. The motivation is not, "God, I need to be a good Christian to impress You today." The motivation is, "God, lead me. I get to live life with You today!" We don't deserve this grace, but it becomes the root of our peace. Every day we trust in Jesus and are reminded how good the gospel is because we get to live life loved by Him and genuinely resting in Him! We will be resting; it will be an adventure of a lifetime! The wild blue yonder is calling! It's God's grace.

The other passage that inspired "The Great Adventure" is Ephesians 2:4-10. The truths are rich.

One could camp out in Ephesians 2:4-10 for quite a while and never want to leave. On this journey with Him, He puts us in the most secure place we could ever be, "seated with Christ." Our majestic views are of His "immeasurable riches of his grace in kindness toward us in Christ Jesus" (verse 7). When we follow where He leads, God will take us to beyond any place we could ever dream or imagine.

If I try to do it my own way, in my own strength, with my own long-faced religious performance, I will not enjoy the great adventure God prepares. There may be some victories along the way. And I'm not saying that life will always be miserable. I still had some great spiritual moments in my early years before I understood grace. But something changes when we grasp the overwhelming love of God. He does something that blows our minds, and, yes, our motivation for living changes!

In the well-known story of the prodigal son in Luke 15, Jesus reveals this idea.

Most of you know this story, but I will give a brief synopsis. The story is of a younger son, who, impatient and greedy, asked his father for his inheritance. Essentially, the younger son wanted to do things his way.

Of course, that doesn't work! The father agreed, but the son blew all his money and eventually became homeless and hopeless, even desiring to eat the same slop the pigs were eating! The son decided to come home and, to his great joy, was welcomed back by his father and brother.

The story often centers on the son we consider the prodigal and how God's love and forgiveness are available when we repent of our selfish ways and return to Him. I've also heard many great sermons about the older son and how he represented the Pharisees of the day. He was jealous of the homecoming of the younger son and fought with the pride of his supposed goodness.

However, the greatest truth might be the analysis of the father. The father, a representative of God, displayed forgiveness and benevolence the younger son did not deserve, yet he gave it. The father's gracious acts rested on his love for his son and that he was a merciful father. It goes beyond that. What did the father do in the story when he saw his son returning? He ran!

He ran to greet his son! In his book, *The Prodigal God,* Tim Keller dared to believe God is the actual prodigal in this parable. We think of "prodigal" as running away and doing bad stuff or making bad decisions. I've always thought that "prodigal" essentially means "wayward." However, more specifically, it means reckless, recklessly extravagant, or "having spent everything." (XIX)

The father ran to his son when his son didn't deserve it. He spent recklessly, killing the fatted calf, and prepared a feast! He gave his son the best robe and put rings and shoes on him, so his son would be ornately dressed. The father was the one who recklessly spent to show his love!

All this takes place for one who didn't deserve it. Remember that the father represents our heavenly Father! Do you see it? He gives us everything! He gave us His life so that we could have salvation. And, He continues to provide us with His life every day so we can live a great adventure in Him!

The more I understand God's amazing grace, the more I want to be on the trail with Him each day of my life. I get to live life not by my might but by trusting in the strength and grace of my Savior.

I don't know where it might lead. I'm sure it will involve proclaiming and worshiping Him while doing things I never dreamed I could do in my own strength. Here is what I do know: wherever it leads, it will be the greatest adventure imaginable because it will be riding with the God of all creation. Yes, the gospel really is that good!

So what do you say? Let's go! With God as our leader, we find the grace that gives our life meaning. Let's follow Him into the glorious unknown!

-Ashley

REFERENCED VERSES

- Luke 15:11-32
- Romans 3:23; 11:36
- 1 Corinthians 2:9

FOR FURTHER STUDY

- *Be the Donkey: Out of the Epicenter,* Kimberly RB Johnson
- *Between Heaven and the Real World: My Story,* Steven Curtis Chapman with Ken Abraham
- *Discover Your Riches in Christ* Lee C. Turner
- *Pilgrim's Progress,* John Bunyan
- (*https://www.gutenberg.org/files/131/131-h/131-h.htm*)
- *The Prodigal God: Recovering the Heart of the Christian Faith,* Timothy Keller
- *The Overcoming Life,* D. L. Moody
- (*https://www.gutenberg.org/files/33015/33015-h/33015-h.htm*)
- *The Rest of the Gospel: When the Partial Gospel Has Worn You Out,* Dan Stone

LIZ HUMOR

©Liz King

THEOLOGY OF SURRENDER:

WHAT IF I STUMBLE?

LIZ HUMOR

© Liz King

DC TALK GOES GRUNGE

It was 1995 and I was chillin' in Compuserve chat rooms when I heard some buzz that my fave rap group, dc Talk, was ditchin' rap for grunge. Dude, I was straight-up buggin'! "Psyche!" I thought to my 14-year-old self. I tried to rationalize away those janky thoughts to comfort myself. But then I read an interview where Toby talked about liking alt-rock and I was like, "Word?!"

But I wasn't gonna let that get me down. I busted out my Josh McDowell reasoning skills and was like, "Toby doesn't sing, he raps! They love rap music—always have, always will!" Those totally wretched rumors were lies from the devil, and I ain't down with that. I'm down with the dc Talk.

Then in the summer of '95, my youth group hit up AtlantaFest at Six Flags Over Georgia, with 4HIM, Newsboys, Steven Curtis Chapman, and the one and only Christian RAP group, dc Talk. I was hyped to see my boys again and hoped the rumors were just that.

I thought I still had more time before I had to find out wassup.

Not!

The night of dc Talk's performance at AtlantaFest was slammin'. I can remember my view of the amphitheater stage and which SCC shirt I had chosen for the special occasion. My True Love Waits ring was gleaming in the setting sun. Everything was still alright in the world. DCT was in the house, boyyyy.

We blissfully watched dc Talk take the stage and perform some of our favorites. Then, "Pow!" dc Talk dropped a bomb on us, announcing they had something new they wanted to perform from their soon-to-be-released next album.

Oh snap. This is it. I began sweating bullets in the Atlanta heat, but my blood ran cold. "Be strong in the Lord, dang it!" I told myself. I needed a side hug.

Then it started. They announced the song. It's called... "Jesus Freak."

I felt adrift. My eyesight started getting blurry. I was vulnerable and exposed. Somebody throw me a soap on a rope to cling to!

It began. What was that? Did I just hear an electric guitar? This was different, edgy, and loud. I was thinking of a way to explain-o. I didn't know how I was supposed to feel, but I knew that what I was hearing was something historic. I was witnessing something I would never forget.

Then it hit me. I stood with a new realization: I. AM. A. JESUS FREAK.

Do you remember the moment you first heard "Jesus Freak"? What did you think?

We asked our followers on social media to tell us about the first time they heard the song or album:

It was at Six Flags. They debuted it on a summer concert tour. It was so different from Free at Last, and I loved it. I was 12, and while my dad listened to White Heart and other Christian rock, "Jesus Freak" felt like it was mine. First song I remember headbanging to. - @differentlaw on Twitter

November 21st 1995. I was a freshman in college and drove straight to Berean Christian bookstore outside of Cincinnati. I played the cassette so much it was ruined within 3 months. - @mrwaggs on Twitter

Hearing the single after wearing out Free at Last blew my mind with the genre change. None of my favorites get their level of notoriety without Jesus Freak existing. - @spsandridge on Twitter

I was in middle school with an older friend at the youth leader's house. I thought, "Wow, what is this sound??" - @NathanWP59206 on Twitter

I saw dc Talk at Sonshine Festival in Wilmar, MN, during the summer of 1995. They played "Jesus Freak" and "In the Light" from their upcoming album. I was hooked. They sold a single of "Jesus Freak" with the wild 60s bubble letter artwork different from the one put in the stores. - @CalCallison on Twitter

Had really been into Free at Last. Heard a new album was dropping. Saw the cassette tape at the Christian bookstore. "I got something for you man..." never been the same since. - @nathanbritt5 on Twitter

Listening station in a Lifeway store. The riff dropped and I threw the headphones off. LOL. It scared my little Baptist brain to death. - @adrianmathenia

It was New Year's Day 1996, was over at the house of some ROTC friends and one of them got it for Christmas. Growing up in a Southern Gospel house, the most "rock" I was allowed to listen to was Carman. Felt like a rebel. - @Adk0n77 on Twitter

My 19 yo self nabbed the single when it first dropped and was quickly "mind blown" at how different it was to Free at Last and, yet, still oh-so-dope. Drove around for an hour straight playing the single package and I think I was literally high from it (the music). - @edifactory on Twitter

My dad worked Graham crusades for years. After one tour, he brought back Jesus Freak (dc Talk was on the tour) and gave it to me secretly in his office, telling me that I would love it, but to not tell my mom because she'd hate it. I listened to it on repeat. - @HamiltonBrbr on Twitter

I wasn't allowed to buy the tape because it was "too worldly" and eventually heard it at a friend's house and thought it was pretty cool despite the fact that I don't think I heard the full album for another 3-5 years. @Tatooed_Llama on Twitter

The hair on my arms stood up. "This is WILD." I thought, "Doesn't sound anything like Free at Last, but I LOVE IT." - @2ToneBlueBlood on Twitter

I caught a snippet of the single on our local Christian radio station (RadioU in Columbus). I lost my mind, found a blank cassette tape, and started waiting for the song to come on so I could record a copy for myself. Took me a week. - @DegenerateTBone on Twitter

My friend had loaned me Bloom a week before and it was…pretty hardcore, ya know. So when he passed me Jesus Freak under the table in Bible class, I think it burned my fingers a little. I think I made it to the title track and immediately turned it off. But eventually came back. - @ryanbrymer on Twitter

Bought the CD with my 15th birthday money. I liked them from Free at Last, so I was expecting more happy, high energy pop. Never listened to Christian radio, so I had no idea they were switching up their sound. I was stunned when I skipped to track 3 and that crunch kicked in. - @johnnygamble on Twitter

I was 18, working on staff at a Bible camp. We were all excited about the rumors that a Christian band made a song that could be played on the Top 40 station. Someone brought the CD and we played it as loud as we could on the chapel sound system. We never tired of it. - @KevinPinball on Twitter

I was at Family Christian Store in early December 2015. Somehow I was one of the only people that hadn't yet heard the song, so when I saw they had a listening station I seized the opportunity. Instantly I knew something was different and this was gonna be special. Everything was so sonic and so crisp and then… "I saw a man with a tat on his big fat belly…" came blaring through the headphones and honestly I peed myself a little. Music and life would never be the same for me since that day to present. I have made dc Talk my favorite group of all time. - @daniellarussois-goingtofight on Instagram

I loved it. The song was great but the album was even better. Total classic. I still call it the "Sgt. Pepper" of CCM to this day. - Louie Tibbs on Facebook

Our youth group bought the single on cassette. One day during our commons time, our youth leader plugged it into the boombox. I stopped what I was doing, being drawn inexplicably toward it. I sat down by the machine and listened intently until it stopped. I then asked my youth pastor if I could buy it, like this copy, right now. She smiled, laughed and said very politely, "No." I was crushed…but she told me where I could get it, and I did as soon as my parents were able to take me to the music store. My dad was appalled at the style of the music, but conceded since it was technically "Christian." But he made the addendum: "I don't want to hear it blaring while I'm around." - NJ Hood on Facebook

Was in church and I remember thinking "I found my anthem." - Jeremy Alan Putman on Facebook

On a school bus headed out to cheer at a late night basketball game. Our school was insanely strict and I wasn't supposed to be listening to such "harsh" music but I was OBSESSED! Thankfully it was a long drive to the game so I sat in the back, hunched down, and threw my headphones on backwards so my hair would hide my crazy music coming from my new CD player. The ride back I had the entire thing memorized. - Hannah West on Facebook

I was driving my cherry red 1989 Ford Probe home from my high school in a suburb of Detroit. I was already a huge dc Talk fan…so when it was played on the secular radio station I turned my volume all the way up. Blowing one of my speakers. Oops. I immediately drove to Best Buy to buy the album in CD. I listened to that CD so many times. Nearly 30 years later I still have that album on CD & still blast it - much to my 18 yr old's dismay (I secretly think she likes it.) - Ashley Suzanne on Facebook

Even CCM artists remember the first time…

> GMA week…the year they released the album. I recall Charlie Peacock came out and sang "In the Light" with them. Seems like Larry Norman was there, too. But when they played "Jesus Freak," I turned to our drummer @spencesmith and said, "We are in!" Up to that point, Christian radio was reluctant to add Big Tent Revival to their playlists, because they thought we were too edgy. Which is funny to think now. But when we heard "Jesus Freak," we knew the radio programmers had to add us. Simply because they can't play Twila Paris and Wayne Watson next to that! That song was not only a hit for dc Talk. It was a hit for a whole genre of music and a whole army of musicians who could now get exposure on the radio. GenX was now in power. - Steve Wiggins from Big Tent Revival @Wigbone on Instagram

As time has marched on, it's clear that *Free at Last* and *Jesus Freak* are both masterpieces in their own right. These guys, self-proclaimed as "two honks and a negro," somehow made it work with this new style. It suited them so well, maybe even better than before.

Now as an adult looking back at the entire dc Talk discography, it's striking that they didn't fit into any one genre. They were their own genre, simply Toby, Michael, and Kevin. No other band could ever replicate what made them so special together. Let me "say the words" that many 90s Christian feel: We love you, dc Talk! Your music inspired us to find our inner Jesus Freak, and for that we're forever grateful.

- Rachel

"I'LL LEAD YOU HOME"

(1995)

Songwriters: Michael W. Smith and Wayne Kirkpatrick

Artist: Michael W. Smith

Album: *I'll Lead You Home*

John 10:27-28–My sheep hear my voice, and I know them, and they follow me. I give them eternal life, and they will never perish, and no one will snatch them out of my hand.

Romans 8:14–For all who are led by the Spirit of God are sons of God.

1 Thessalonians 5:23-24–Now may the God of peace himself sanctify you completely, and may your whole spirit and soul and body be kept blameless at the coming of our Lord Jesus Christ. He who calls you is faithful; he will surely do it.

90S IMPRESSION

God extends to us the call of the gospel, and in that call, we accept Him and find salvation and eternal life in Heaven.

TODAY'S IMPRESSION

The call of God is not only to salvation but to sanctification. God speaks and leads each day, and our trust in Him brings continual direction in our personal spiritual growth until we finally reach eternity.

The opening lyrics of Smitty's "I'll Lead You Home" resonate like a Davidic psalm. You know, the ones in which David began with all the bad stuff? He was wandering and desperately feeling adrift. Yet, amid David's dark place, he cried out to God, knowing Who will lead him home. God is our refuge and shield and the light that brightens our path. We must leave it to Him, for He is our only hope to arrive safely home.

Are you a born again Christian, yet still find yourself wandering? If so, the lyrics of "I'll Lead You Home" may strike a chord. Salvation is yours, but you often find yourself running aimlessly.

Fear grips you, and at times you might even question your salvation. Are you going to make it? And if so, how? Surely God did not save us for mere fire insurance only to expect us to fend for ourselves in the Christian journey toward our eternal home.

The title track of Michael W. Smith's Grammy Award-winning album *I'll Lead You Home* prompts the believer who is now "in Christ" to do something vital in the Christian walk. Listen to His voice! He's leading us somewhere. I believe that He is leading us toward our sanctification.

In the devotion "In Christ Alone," we discussed salvation by grace through faith alone. No amount of spiritual performance or religion earns our salvation. It is solely the work of God as we put faith in Him. Furthermore, He seals us in the Holy Spirit. Salvation is the gift of a regenerated heart in rebirth; if God does the work of redemption, he will not "unregenerate" you.

God saves you. So, um, what's next? Good question.

I recall a craft we used in backyard Bible clubs in my early ministry years. We would create multi-colored bead bracelets with the children. Do you remember the order? A black bead represented sin and our need for a Savior. A red stood for Jesus' blood. A white proclaimed the purifying work of our Savior in salvation. A blue symbolized baptism. A green bead taught young Christians the need for spiritual growth. A gold bead reminded us of Heaven.

I remember teaching children their new "spiritual checklist," based on the green bead. Read your Bible. Pray. Worship and go to church. Witness. Growth as a Christian (often referred to as sanctification) is on us, right?

Inconsistent spiritual growth and doubt frequent the lives of many seasoned Christians. Sanctification can be debilitating for many Christians as they feel all the work is on them. Unfortunately, though not surprisingly, they keep blowing it. In reality, God is just as much a part of the sanctifying as He is of the justifying. Just how does God sanctify us?

Sanctification means "set apart." God alone sets us apart in sanctification by making us holy. Only God can make us holy. It is His work, yet we surrender to what He wants us to do. God undoubtedly wants us to be active in spiritual disciplines. He calls us to sanctification and holy living, and we are to respond to His call and trust Him. Our response to Jesus will entail various Christian "exercises." The spiritual things we do are the fruit of who we are. God does the growing.

As we seek to understand the issue of sanctification and the lyrics of the MWS song, take a look at Romans 8.

Paul's theological discourse and promises in Romans 8 might entail the best and most exciting chapter in the Bible. Think about it. We escape condemnation if we are in Christ (See verse 1 and the following.). We are free from the law of sin and death (verse 2). The law cannot save us, but Jesus can (verse 3). God causes all things to work together for good to those who love Him and are called by Him (verse 28). If God is for us, who can stand against us (verse 31)? Jesus intercedes for us (verse 34). Nothing can separate us from His love (verse 35). No matter what comes our way, we are more than conquerors through Him who loved us (verses 37-39).

And the heart of the chapter continually reminds us of the working of the Spirit in our lives. The Spirit who raised Jesus from the dead gives us life (See Romans 8:11.). He testifies to us that we are His children (verses 15-17). He gives us hope (verses 24-25). He helps us in our weaknesses (verse 26).

Amid all of those incredible truths is the mystery of sanctification. "For all who are led by the Spirit of God are sons of God" (Romans 8:14). Of course, sons generally means "children," including daughters, in this context.

God speaks to His children. Our job is to listen and follow.

Growth takes place by listening to the leading of the Spirit. Not only does He lead, He also empowers us as we trust. Imagine the same Spirit that raised Jesus from the dead now lives in us. The prophet Isaiah reminded us that He is speaking and directing (See Isaiah 30:21.). How are we sanctified? We are sanctified by attending to God's voice and acting on what He says.

Scripture clearly says we are to set our minds on the Spirit and fix our eyes on Christ. When our focus is on Him, He directs our steps.

We must turn it all over to the Savior, who, by His very own choice, gave His life to us. He is able! The apostle Paul stated in 1 Thessalonians 5:23-24 that God is the one who sanctifies. He is faithful and will do it completely. Therefore, we must listen and trust Him and act on what He says. Do you hear Him calling? He wants to lead you home!

He not only calls us to salvation. He gets us home.

In his classic work *Of the Mortification of Sin in Believers,* John Owen asserted,

> There is, if I may so say, a secret instinct in faith, whereby it knows the voice of Christ when he speaks indeed; as the babe leaped in the womb when the blessed Virgin came to Elisabeth, faith leaps in the heart when Christ indeed draws nigh to it. "My sheep," says Christ, "know my voice." (Chapter XIII)

In my first semester in seminary, I recall my New Testament professor explaining how sheep know their shepherd's voice. My professor shared how, while in the Holy Land, he witnessed a shepherd approaching a barn that housed various sheep as they lodged for the night. In the morning, the door was open, and the shepherd began to sing a song. One by one, single file, the sheep exited the barn, following their shepherd's voice.

The shepherd led them. He protected them. Yes, he made sure they grew strong as he led them toward refreshing water and green pastures.

The sheep's job? Listen and go where the shepherd leads. When arriving at a stream, drink. Be nurtured in His Word. Rest in His arms. Worship Him as you follow His voice.

God's children will hear the calling of His Spirit. He will lead us to bountiful pastures of growth that will be far more sanctifying than anything we can muster up. He will lead us to moral and holy living as we are His representatives to the world. Jesus made us His sheep and keeps working on us. And He who began a good work in us will be faithful to complete it!

We have been made new and are in a new righteous standing. So, stand there!

Observing what Christ has accomplished, we realize that His accomplishment was not only our salvation. He remains in us each moment of every day as our Guide. He wants to grow us and set us apart for sanctification. As He empowers, we are to act like who we are!

Trust the leading of your Shepherd. He holds the keys to your righteousness. And truthfully, this idea of sanctification is a struggle for many Christians. Do not lose heart! Remember that God is the one who makes you holy, and surrender to Him!

Do you have a troubled mind? a doubter's heart? Be encouraged because you are not alone!

He's calling. Follow. He wants to lead you home!

- Ashley

REFERENCED VERSES

- Isaiah 30:21
- John 3; 10:27-28
- Romans 5:11; 8
- Ephesians 1; 2:8-9
- Philippians 1:6
- 1 Thessalonians 5:23-24
- Hebrews 12:1-3

FOR FURTHER STUDY

- *How the Gospel Brings Us All the Way Home*, Derek W. H.Thomas
- *Overcoming Sin and Temptation: Three Classic Works by John Owen*, Edited by Kelly M. Kapic and Justin Taylor
- *Of the Mortification of Sin*, John Owen (*https://ccel.org/ccel/owen/mort/mort.i.i.html*)

"I SURRENDER ALL"

(1993)

Songwriters: Reginald Glenn Hamm and David E. Moffitt

Artist: Clay Crosse

Album: *My Place is With You*

> **Matthew 16:24-26**–Then Jesus told his disciples, "If anyone would come after me, let him deny himself and take up his cross and follow me. For whoever would save his life will lose it, but whoever loses his life for my sake will find it. For what will it profit a man if he gains the whole world and forfeits his soul? Or what shall a man give in return for his soul?"

> **James 1:4**–And let steadfastness have its full effect, that you may be perfect and complete, lacking in nothing.

90S IMPRESSION

We must surrender all to Jesus.

TODAY'S IMPRESSION

We must surrender all to Jesus, and in return, we receive Jesus and His kingdom.

There's an elephant in the room. Clay Crosse's first name isn't Clay, nor is his last name Crosse. Get ready for it: He's actually Walter Clayton Crossnoe. You down with WCC? Yeah, you know me.

If you can sing WC^2's hit song, "I Surrender All" without a line or two from Mark Lowry's "I Can Eat It All" parody sneaking in, then you are better than I am. It gets me every time! While one has me thinking of hamburgers and fries, the other causes serious contemplation on what I am clinging to in my life–both good and bad. You can probably tell which is which.

Let's get to it. Take a moment to listen to the crooning Crossnoe.

The lyrics recall the story of Abraham and his beloved son, Isaac. In Genesis 22, God spoke to Abraham and asked him to do the unthinkable–sacrifice his son for a burnt offering. When I ponder this unthinkable request, I can't even imagine the awkward dinner conversations years later. "Dad, remember the day when you were going to sacrifice me? Good times!" God's plan was beyond their scope.

This was a test, and it wasn't easy. In *The Pursuit of God*, Preacher A.W. Tozer suggested,

> The sacred writer spares us a close-up of the agony that night on the slopes of Beersheba when the aged man had it out with his God, but respectful imagination may view in awe the bent form and convulsive wrestling alone under the stars. Possibly not again until a Greater than Abraham wrestled in the Garden of Gethsemane did such a mortal pain visit a human soul.

As we know so well, Abraham obeyed and God intervened at the very last moment to save Isaac. God provided a ram, which was offered in the son's place. There on Mt. Moriah, we see an early picture of the gospel.

Tozer taught that God will "sooner or later bring us to this test." The result of testing is steadfastness leading to maturity and godliness. He calls surrender the "spiritual secret," the "sweet theology of the heart" that can't be taught in books (See James 1:4.).

Our testing begins at the moment of our salvation. Asking us to consider the cost of discipleship, Jesus Himself commanded us to take up our cross and follow Him:

> For whoever would save his life will lose it, but whoever loses his life for my sake will find it. For what will it profit a man if he gains the whole world and forfeits his soul? Or what shall a man give in return for his soul? (Matthew 16:25-26).

Complete relinquishment of self is not a suggestion. It is a prerequisite to following after Jesus.

Surrender is not without its reward. Look what we receive in turn: Jesus and His kingdom! In Matthew 13, Jesus told several parables to describe the kingdom of Heaven. In one, Jesus described the kingdom as a treasure found hidden in a field. The man who finds it sells all he has to purchase that field. In another parable, Jesus illustrated the kingdom as like a merchant who finds a valuable pearl. He sells all he has to purchase it. The kingdom is worth all we have to give.

As such, we are called to be more than mere stewards of temporary earthly blessings. Rather, we are called to be inheritors of His eternal kingdom (See Matthew 25:34.). Are we working hard to build our kingdoms when we should be serving in His?

At least on Earth, surrender is a lifelong, everyday process. It's a never-ending examination and prayer. We sing the song and have to start right back over again. Sometimes we succeed, sometimes we fail. His love remains.

When we think about surrender, we envision the posture of both hands raised in the air. The recognized sign of surrender means to give up. As Christians, are we giving up? You'd better believe it! We give up and wholly put our trust in Christ.

Our joy is that we do this *with* and *for* King Jesus, who knows exactly what it is to surrender all–for God's glory and our salvation. We fix our eyes on Him as He works in us to make us more like Him (See Hebrews 12:2.). Let's pray Tozer's prayer together:

> Father, I want to know Thee, but my coward heart fears to give up its toys. I cannot part with them without inward bleeding, and I do not try to hide from Thee the terror of the parting. I come trembling, but I do come. Please root from my heart all those things which I have cherished so long and which have become a very part of my living self, so that Thou mayest enter and dwell there without a rival. Then shalt Thou make the place of Thy feet glorious. Then shall my heart have no need of the sun to shine in it, for Thyself wilt be the light of it, and there shall be no night there. In Jesus' name, Amen.

Lord, help us to surrender all to You for Your glory and kingdom.

- Rachel

REFERENCED VERSES

- Genesis 22
- Matthew 13; 16:24-26; 25:34
- Hebrews 12:2
- James 1:4

FOR FURTHER STUDY

- *Out of a Far Country: A Gay Son's Journey to God. A Broken Mother's Search for Hope*, Christopher Yuan and Angela Yuan

- *Simply Jesus: A New Vision of Who He Was, What He Did, and Why It Matters,* N.T. Wright
- *The Pursuit of God,* A.W. Tozer
  (*https://www.gutenberg.org/ebooks/25141*)

"WHERE THERE IS FAITH"

(1990)

Songwriter: Billy Simon

Artist: 4HIM

Album: *4HIM*

John 20:29–Jesus said to him, "Have you believed because you have seen me? Blessed are those who have not seen and yet have believed."

2 Corinthians 5:7–For we walk by faith, not by sight.

Hebrews 11:1–Now faith is the assurance of things hoped for, the conviction of things not seen.

1 Peter 1:8-9–Though you have not seen him, you love him. Though you do not now see him, you believe in him and rejoice with joy that is inexpressible and filled with glory, obtaining the outcome of your faith, the salvation of your souls.

90S IMPRESSION

If I can just have enough faith, I'll be OK. Faith is totally blind. Faith is a spiritual merit badge I wear to show God I am His.

TODAY'S IMPRESSION

The ability to have faith is another one of God's gifts of grace to us. Faith is not a totally blind guessing game. Faith is based on the person and character of God. The question to ask is not, "Do I have enough faith?" The correct question is, "Who is my faith in?"

The idea of faith can easily become a misunderstood case of "Christianese," which the lost world might not understand. We must be crucified, justified, sanctified, washed in the blood, and have faith. (I recall seeing a good 90s skit involving Christianese!) But that is just what Christians do. They walk by faith. So, what does walking by faith mean?

Yes, faith is "the assurance of things hoped for, the conviction of things not seen." In this introductory verse in the Hebrews 11 Faith Hall of Fame, the writer made it clear. When you have faith, you receive assurance. The substance of your faith contains conviction in something you might not have seen. Still, you believe.

Studying the great biblical characters in Hebrews 11 led me to some interesting conclusions: The heroes of faith had faith in what seemed to be unseen. However, their faith was not blind. Each placed their faith in the character and promises of God. Also, believing in Him is much more than believing things *about* Him.

We can believe in many things and not have faith. We can believe in peace and love. Honesty and trust are good things in which to hold fast. Nevertheless, they are not enough. We can believe in all these things and even possess a lot of wishful thinking. In *The Case for Hope,*

Lee Strobel put it out there, commenting, "Wishful thinking doesn't change reality." (8) He's right. What I think and hope doesn't change anything about anything without faith.

Faith is a necessity. And faith must be in the person of Jesus Christ. In another apologetic work, *The Case for the Real Jesus*, Strobel stated, "Faith is only as good as the one in whom it's invested." (10) But, we struggle because Jesus was on Earth over 2,000 years ago, and we weren't there to see Him and touch Him.

People often muse, "If I could have been on Earth when Jesus was here and seen Him with my own eyes, I would believe." Or, "If only I witnessed Jesus performing miracles, interacting with His disciples, helping people, and really coming back from the dead, I then might consider Him to be God." Sadly, many people observed all of those things, yet still didn't believe. Seeing undoubtedly encourages our faith and helps us overcome obstacles in our growth. However, seeing is not believing. Seeing engages our brains, but faith captures our hearts.

In a sermon entitled "Faith: What Is It? How Can it Be Obtained?" 19th-century pastor Charles Spurgeon commented, "Faith occupies the position of a channel or conduit-pipe. Grace is the fountain and the stream: Faith is the aqueduct along which the flood of mercy flows down to refresh the thirsty sons of men."

We come to God thirsty with parched tongues, hoping for a drink. Faith in Christ brings hope to reality, and a wellspring of eternal life quenches our spiritual thirst. This is possible as hope in Christ is living hope!

There is even a noteworthy difference between being amazed by something and having faith. Emotions are not life-changing faith and trust. Believing in your heart goes beyond a feeling, and yes, clear evidence that might even be right in front of your face. Captivation and amazement are often steps in the process of faith, but they do not equal the substance of faith. In the same sermon, Spurgeon perceived what makes up faith–*knowledge, belief, and trust.*

Imagine observing thrill-seekers skydive out of an airplane and into the Grand Canyon. The magnificence of the entire event moves you. Person after person jumps out and flies like an eagle over the breathtaking creation of God, landing safely on the canyon floor. They enthusiastically say it was the greatest experience of their life. Now, will you do what they did, and put on your parachute, jump, and believe you will be OK? Do you trust the parachute?

After being asked to see His nail-scarred hands by Thomas, Jesus stated, and even questioned, in John 20:29, "Have you believed because you have seen me? Blessed are those who have not seen and yet have believed." The Bible states that faith is not based on empirical evidence but on divine assurance and is a gift of God (See Ephesians 2:8.). God gives us knowledge of Him when we trust in the miracle of grace. Grace does what we can't do, so our choice is obvious. We believe.

I love empirical evidence as much as the next guy! I love to study it, teach it in defending the truth of the gospel and God's Word, and see how it really can captivate our minds and strengthen our beliefs. Seeing is a good thing. It is one of the best things! Still, seeing is not believing. And to quote another 4HIM title, when you look at the entire biblical narrative and study prophetic truths about God and His Word, you "Can't Get Past the Evidence."

Faith is a byproduct of trusting in who God says He is, and believing, though not always seeing, that He is the ultimate truth. Where that faith exists, assurance comes flowing in divine fountains!

I fear that, too often, people confuse head knowledge with heart knowledge. You can recognize all the right "stuff" about Jesus and still be lost. Do you know Him? Have you trusted Him with your life? Surrendering your life to Jesus reaches far beyond religion, morality, or believing empirical data. None of these things equate to faith.

However, when the Spirit enlightens us to the truth of the person of Jesus, and we trust Him with our lives, something happens! As you rest in the assurance of His grace and enter into a relationship with

Him by faith, you begin to see more than ever before. Strap the parachute on, and jump!

God is not satisfied with us merely being awestruck or emotional or knowing all the correct answers to the most critical questions. He is not impressed in the least with our religion. He wants to live and rule in our hearts. Hebrews 11:6 states that God works so that we will "believe that he exists and that he rewards those who seek him."

Where there is faith, the voice of God leads. Where there is faith in Christ, a weary traveler is never alone. Where there is faith, unspeakable peace comforts weary souls.

Faith in Christ leads to one who will carry my burdens. He carried them all the way to the cross. Faith leads to hope everlasting.

There is no burden too big or hurt too deep that is too big for faith. That truth is a reality because of the One my trust is in, and He is alive!

Jesus has done what you needed to do and could not do, so you could trust in what He did and wants to do in your life. Put your faith in Him today. Your eyes will see as your heart is enlightened. Where there is faith in Christ, you will be amazed. There is no better place to be!

- Ashley

REFERENCED VERSES

- John 20:29
- 2 Corinthians 5:7
- Ephesians 2:8
- Hebrews 11
- 1 Peter 1:8-9

FOR FURTHER STUDY

- "Faith: What Is It? How Can it Be Obtained?" Charles Spurgeon
- (*https://www.spurgeon.org/resource-library/sermons/faith-what-is-it-how-can-it-be-obtained/#flipbook/*)
- *In a Pit with a Lion on a Snowy Day: How to Survive and Thrive When Opportunity Roars*, Mark Batterson
- *The Case for Faith: A Journalist Investigates the Toughest Objections to Christianity,* Lee Strobel
- *The Case for Hope: Looking Ahead with Confidence and Courage,* Lee Strobel
- *The Case for the Real Jesus: A Journalist Investigates Current Attacks on the Identity of Christ,* Lee Strobel

"ADDICTED TO JESUS"

(1991)

Songwriters: Joseph Randolph Hogue, Carman Licciardello, and Toby McKeehan

Artist: Carman

Album: *Addicted to Jesus*

> **Ecclesiastes 2:10-11**–Whatever my eyes desired I did not keep from them. I kept my heart from no pleasure, for my heart found pleasure in all my toil, and this was my reward for all my toil. Then I considered all that my hands had done and the toil I had expended in doing it, and behold, all was vanity and a striving after wind, and there was nothing to be gained under the sun.

> **Ecclesiastes 12:13-14**–The end of the matter; all has been heard. Fear God and keep his commandments, for this is the whole duty of man. For God will bring every deed into judgment, with every secret thing, whether good or evil.

Matthew 6:19-21–"Do not lay up for yourselves treasures on earth, where moth and rust destroy and where thieves break in and steal, but lay up for yourselves treasures in heaven, where neither moth nor rust destroys and where thieves do not break in and steal. For where your treasure is, there your heart will be also."

90S IMPRESSION

We need to love Jesus the most, above all else.

TODAY'S IMPRESSION

Still true! Furthermore, if Jesus is not what we love the most, we can be sure that something else sits in that sacred place.

Feeling A to J? Thanks to this Carman jam featuring a rambunctious performance from your boyz Toby, Michael, and Kevin, we have a question that only makes sense to 90s Christian peeps. It's like a secret code. If someone answers with a resounding "Yes!", you know you've found a new best friend to kick the ballistics with or whatnot.

This song can be more than just a good time. Carman asked a very important question that gets to the very heart of what it means to follow after Christ: Are you addicted to Jesus? It's an interesting turn of phrase to use the word "addicted" to describe the relationship with our Lord, but I think it works. Let's break it down.

As humans, we have a dependency problem. In ways big and small, we are all reliant upon something or someone. Even a newborn baby understands its dependency problem when it cries out for comfort, food, and other basic needs. You know how it goes. We are always jonesing for something.

This is not only evident for our physical bodies, but our hearts are also just as needy. Eighteenth-century Puritan preacher Thomas Chalmers suggests that the heart's greatest need is an object that it can love deeply and intensely. He taught that without something to love, we would have "a void and a vacancy as painful to the mind as hunger is to the natural system. It may be deprived of one object, or of any, but it cannot be emptied of all." (*Expulsive Power of a New Affection*)

A heart without an object to love is analogous to a starving body without sustenance. Like an empty stomach, a heart cannot exist empty for long. According to Chalmers, our heart may develop new affections or switch to different ones, but it cannot remain empty. To leave a heart hollow is to bring about "the most intolerable suffering." Naturally, our hearts seek something worthy for which to give affection to stop those heart-hunger pains.

Our hearts must bestow its affections on something. You could say, we are addicted to loving something. We can't live without something that makes us want to get up in the morning: something to drive us to do that which is hard, something to live for.

What then? Should we consider this inner necessity a design flaw or a result of the fall? Should we be like the Buddhists and try to rid ourselves of all desire? Will this ease our suffering?

I think not. Can you imagine not having desire or love for anything? An all-encompassing absence of interest is a sign of depression often accompanied by fatigue, restlessness, and overall misery. When a heart stops beating for something, it no longer cares to beat. Left untreated, this depth of depression can steal a life. Our hearts were not designed to be devoid of passion, desire, and love. Living as an empty shell is not the abundant life He wants to give us (See John 10:10.).

Even before the fall, humans were dependent upon Him for life and goodness, and the Father did not hold back His goodness. In Genesis 2, we see that Adam was given a helpmate, for it was not good for him to be alone. Together, they received a lush, beautiful garden from which to live and eat, the plentiful tree of life to give wellness, an identity as image bearers, and a unique intimacy with their King. They need Him, and He gives them what they need. He called that good (See Genesis 1:31.). Our heart's God-given ability to need can draw us closer to Him and bring about fulfillment and joy as we experience His goodness.

What happens when we want what we don't need and need what we don't want? Genesis 3 royally messed up everything, didn't it? In "Addicted to Jesus," Carman lyrically lists a few of the endless ways in which the flesh tries to feed our hungry hearts. Some of these affections, such as exercise, are harmless and even healthy and wonderful gifts from God. Did I just call exercise a gift?

Even so, when compared to the Edenic connection we were originally designed to crave, anything less than Him is unmasked as an absurd imposter unworthy of our deepest devotion. With poetic clarity, the author of Ecclesiastes revealed,

> Whatever my eyes desired I did not keep from them. I kept my heart from no pleasure, for my heart found pleasure in all my toil, and this was my reward for all my toil. Then I considered all that my hands had done and the toil I had expended in doing it, and behold, all was vanity and a striving after wind, and there was nothing to be gained under the sun (2:10-11).

Pursuit of temporary pleasures will prove futile and pointless. The final words of Ecclesiastes direct us to what (or rather Who) should be the center of our affection.

> The end of the matter; all has been heard. Fear God and keep his commandments, for this is the whole duty of man. For God will bring every deed into judgment, with every secret thing, whether good or evil (12:13-14).

Furthermore, Jesus taught us to treasure that which is eternal:

> "Do not store up for yourselves treasures on earth, where moths and vermin destroy, and where thieves break in and steal. But store up for yourselves treasures in Heaven, where moths and

vermin do not destroy, and where thieves do not break in and steal. For where your treasure is, there your heart will be also" (Matthew 6:19-21).

As Chalmers taught, the heart will not beat without something to beat for. If Jesus is not the centerpiece of our hearts, that sacred space does not remain empty. You can be sure that we have filled that void with something else that we deem more worthy and will actively pursue that next temporary fix.

We must ask ourselves the question that was posed to us in the song. Are you addicted to Jesus? What has your heart cultivated as its treasure? Do you see an empire of vanity? Or, do you see Jesus and His kingdom (See Matthew 6:33.)?

As we inventory the addictions of our hearts, what we find might be sobering. As Chalmers revealed, we are called to "exchange an old affection for a new one." With a true dependence on the Spirit, let's trade our love of the things of the world for the love of the Father (See 1 John 2:15.). Feeling A to J?

-Rachel

REFERENCED VERSES

- Genesis 1:31; 3
- Ecclesiastes 2:10-11; 12:13-14
- Matthew 6:19-21; 6:33
- John 10:10
- 1 John 2:15

FOR FURTHER STUDY

- *Born Again This Way: Coming Out, Coming to Faith, and What Comes Next*, Rachel Gilson
- *God Does His Best Work With Empty*, Nancy Guthrie
- *The Expulsive Power of a New Affection*, Thomas Chalmers (*https://www.monergism.com/expulsive-power-new-affection*)

LIZ HUMOR

© Liz King

SUPER SUPERLATIVES

Let's pretend that our favorite CCM artists and bands were part of our high school class. Would any of them be nominated for a yearbook superlative? We think so. If it were up to my (Rachel) daughters, Kevin Max would sweep the board. Who would you choose? Thanks to the fellow mixtape theologians mentioned below for their nominations.

We've got the traditional categories...

- **Most Likely to Succeed: Steven Curtis Chapman** *(Jesse Wilkin and Caralyn Warran-Reil)*

Since releasing his first album *First Hand* in 1987, Steven Curtis Chapman has achieved countless Dove Awards, Grammy Awards, bestselling books, and the most #1 hits of any CCM artist. Additionally, his work in co-founding Show Hope in 2003 with his wife, Mary Beth, has blazed a new trail in caring for orphans here and around the world.

- **Best Dressed: OC Supertones** *(Tauni Jean-Georges)*

This ska band from Orange County formed in 1995. They looked superfly with their coordinating black tailored suits and ties, shades, and chain wallets. They even played in front of Pope John Paul II in 1999.

- **Best Smile: Amy Grant**

During the time when Nashville was considering hosting its own NHL hockey team, television ads were aired to sway public support. One especially effective local ad featured a solitary hockey player in full uniform and mask fiercely skating toward the camera. Right before the mysterious character reached the camera, the player came to a sudden halt, removed the helmet and mask, and revealed a smiling Amy Grant. Needless to say, Nashville got its hockey team. Go Preds.

- **Best Hair: Stryper** *(George Hartz)*

These guys have the shiny, gravity-defying, glorious locks of our dreams. No competition. Enough said.

- **Most Attractive Female: CeCe Winans**

This 15-time Grammy Award-winning lady must have the Benjamin Button's disease. She was voted one of Nashville's "Most Beautiful People" in 2021 by *Nashville Lifestyles Magazine*. With her work with World Vision and numerous other ministries, she radiates beauty from the inside out.

- **Most Attractive Male: Michael W. Smith** *(Jeremy Alan Putnam)*

In 1992, Smitty was listed as one of *People Magazine's* "Most Beautiful People." Mark Lowry hilariously parodied "Place in this World" with "Face in this World," which chronicles the funny man's surgical attempts to achieve Michael's rugged good looks. All class, Michael made a cameo appearance in the music video.

- **Most Popular: dc Talk**

Everyone's favorites, Toby McKeehan, Michael Tait, and Kevin Max, released their first album in 1989 and broke our hearts when they announced their hiatus in 2000. Like a bad breakup, we've been crying in our ice cream ever since.

- **Best Role Model: Rebecca St. James**

Australian-born Rebecca Smallbone took the stage name Rebecca St. James when she released her first US album in 1994 at age 16. With songs like "God," and "Everything I Do," Rebecca was the antithesis of mainstream 90s teen pop princesses. In the 90s, she was a brave voice for abstinence and godly character. Rebecca married her darling, Jacob "Cubbie" Fink, at age 33. You go, girl!

- **Best Personality: Kirk Franklin**

Some people just got "it." The ultimate hype man, the magnetic Mr. Franklin can rally audiences of all backgrounds to stomp and start a revolution.

- **Class Clown: Mark Lowry**

Whether cutting up with jokes in the sanctuary or parodying our favorite CCM songs, this multi-talented poster boy for hyperactivity can make anything funny.

- **Best Friendship: Geoff Moore & Steven Curtis Chapman**
  (*Tabitha Rowley*)

Both excellent songwriters on their own, together these two friends for life have produced some very special tunes. We wouldn't have classics like "The Great Adventure" and "Listen to Our Hearts" without this bromance.

- **Most Artistic: Kevin Max** (*Eliza and Emajean Freeze*)

Always a little mysterious, Kevin is the creative, fantasy-loving kid that writes poetry and paints abstract art. Mr. Vibrato is the artistic mastermind behind the well-loved *Jesus Freak* album cover. Since his dc Talk days, his solo pursuits have been experimental and daring.

- **Most Athletic: Audio Adrenaline**

These playful guys love sports so much that their idea of Heaven is a big house where they can play football.

- **Best Christian Character: Rich Mullins** (*Nathan Ludwick*)

Rich would probably completely shun such a title, and that's why he deserves it. We miss you, Mr. Mullins.

And the not-so-traditional categories...

- **Most Neighborly: Mrs. Morgan**

We were first introduced to Mrs. Morgan in *Jesus Freak,* and we've had a special place in our hearts for this sassy neighbor ever since.

- **Most Likely to Frighten the Parental Units: Mortification**

Pop this in the boombox and you might get some worried looks from mom and dad. Pioneers in Christian death metal, these Australian artists created a much-needed space for this genre. Their music is deep and hard-hitting. We think the parents would come around once they read the lyrics.

- **Most Likely to Cut Class: Switchfoot**

Instead of reading the books, these guys would rather watch the movie. You might find them playing around when they should be studying in Chem 6A.

- **Most "Christian-y" Band Name: Jars of Clay**

Despite the flood of competition, Jars of Clay is the most Christian-y band name of them all, and we love it. Coming straight from 2 Corinthians 4:7, the name helps us remember the treasure of the gospel.

- **Best at Giving Directions: Michael W. Smith** *(Matthew Davis)*

Been roaming through the night? He'll show you which way is west, I mean, best.

- **Most Likely to Get in a Fight: Carman**

Need Satan to bite the dust? Ready to start a R.I.O.T. against the monsters in your house? These enemies don't stand a chance against this charismatic champion. Carman fought the good fight.

Congratulations to all the winners!

"GOD IS IN CONTROL"

(1993)

Songwriter: Twila Paris

Artist: Twila Paris

Album: *Beyond a Dream*

Luke 22:40-44–When he came to the place, he said to them, "Pray that you may not enter into temptation." And he withdrew from them about a stone's throw and knelt and prayed, saying, '"Father, if you are willing, remove this cup from me. Nevertheless, not my will, but yours, be done." And there appeared to him an angel from heaven, strengthening him. And being in agony he prayed more earnestly; and his sweat became like great drops of blood falling down to the ground.

Philippians 4:6-7–Do not be anxious about anything, but in everything by prayer and supplication with thanksgiving let your requests be made known to God. And the peace of God, which surpasses all understanding, will guard your hearts and your minds in Christ Jesus.

90S IMPRESSION

God is in control.

TODAY'S IMPRESSION

Amid the challenges and anxieties in life, I can rest in God's sover-eignty and the promises He gives to His children.

God is in control. How many times have we heard that? We can tell that to other Christians so much that it becomes cliché. They are going through a horrific tragedy, struggling in a dysfunctional home, or possibly battling against crippling anxiety. We tell the person, "God is in control, so everything is going to be OK." The words of comfort come from the right place, but the person is still in despair.

And, that is not to say the statement is incorrect. The sovereignty of God brings great comfort when we are in need, and it is undoubtedly something we need to remind ourselves and others. Yet, telling someone that God is in control while possibly quoting Philippians 4:6-7 may not help them in that precise moment.

Maybe understanding what the statement "God is in control" means, and the realities of Philippians 4:6-7 will bring hope and encourage-ment. And while we are on this subject, what about the issue of anxi-ety? If we feel trapped and emotionally overwhelmed, wondering if we can ever come up for air, are we in sin? Is it a sin to have anxiety?

In her 1993 mega-hit, "God is in Control," Twila Paris provided much-needed insight into this discussion. For starters, we might mention that Twila is quite the songwriter. She made her name in the 80s and in the early 90s. She was as big as they come, winning the Dove Award for female vocalist of the year three years in a row. Country artist Barbara Mandrell famously sang that she (Barbara) was "Country When Country Wasn't Cool." Well, in the days before "Jesus Freak" and "Big

House," Twila was CCM when CCM wasn't as cool. She also has songs in many of our hymn books that many people will recognize: "He Is Exalted," "We Bow Down," "Lamb of God," and "How Beautiful," to name a few.

"God is in Control" is a perfect example of one of those songs we listen to at Mixtape Theology and realize our spiritual and theological growth through the years. Back to that cliché word of advice: God is in control. Someone might respond, "Um, OK. But I'm still struggling."

David Martyn Lloyd-Jones, the great British preacher of the 20th century, gave great insight into the struggle in his work *Spiritual Depression*:

> We must start by understanding that we may well find ourselves in a position by which our faith is going to be tried … If we are living the Christian life, or trying to live the Christian life, at the moment, on the assumption that it means just come to Christ and you will never have any more worry in the whole of your life, we are harboring a terrible fallacy. (140)

It is indeed a fallacy to minimize or deny that worry is not a reality. So what do we do? What, or more specifically who, are we holding onto as we struggle? And remember, the One we are holding on to is holding us. In our worries, realizing who is holding us is incredibly comforting. The God who created the universe by speaking it into existence created us, knows all about us and everything we experience, and holds us. Hold onto Him! He's got you.

I've often thought about Jesus' words in the garden of Gethsemane when he asked His Father to remove the cup from Him. Essentially, Jesus, in His humanity, was struggling with what He was about to face. There was the physical pain of crucifixion and, most notably, the divine wrath of the Father. When Jesus would become sin who knew no sin and faced the wrath of God on our behalf, He faced the grimmest reality possible. As He faced this reality, Luke stated that He sweated great drops of blood as He prayed to His Father.

The medical phenomenon known as hematohidrosis is when one is under such anguish that sweat becomes blood. This rare medical condition occurs when one has not been cut or injured. In His humanity, Jesus experienced it.

Can you imagine? Jesus, the Son of God, was so stressed that He was sweating blood. But stress is what took place. When you think about it, Jesus had anxiety.

So, that answers that question. If the perfect Son of God who never sinned experienced anxiety, we can establish that an anxious Christian is not always in sin. While none of us will ever face the stress that Jesus faced, the truth is, Jesus experienced anxiety. This brings me great comfort when I have days of anxiousness or panic. Jesus knows what that feels like, far beyond what I can imagine. It gives me comfort in the fact that I'm not in sin for feeling those emotions. I must remember who I trust and who will help me.

As Jesus faced God's cup of wrath for our sin, He was faithful to do what God planned. As Jesus stated, "Nevertheless, not my will, but yours, be done," the path was clear (Luke 22:42). Jesus would trust in God amid distress, and we must as well. One of my favorite passages of Scripture is 1 Peter 5:7, which states, "Casting all your anxieties on him, because he cares for you."

We will have anxieties. And what do we do with them? We cast them on Jesus. The Greek word for casting is *epiripto*. This compound word combines *epi*, which means "upon," and *ripto*, which is "to hurl, to throw, or to cast." The meaning of the word would most often entail hurling or violently throwing. When you are casting, you are flinging something away with a great deal of force. Don't place those anxieties down gently. Throw those suckers. Hurl them!

Our sovereign God is aware we will have anxieties, is in control, and desires for us to cast those anxieties to Him. And why does He do this? Because He cares for us! He loves us! God desires for us to trust in Him and His will just as Jesus did as He trusted His heavenly Father. It is not the mere fact that God is in control. God is in control, has experienced what we experience, is sharing it with us, cares for us, and wants us to know He is there.

Even if you aren't feeling God's presence at the moment, by faith, continue to cry out to a God who is there. In your anxieties, you can rest assured that you may feel forsaken but will never be abandoned. Persecutions will not be stronger than the shield of faith you carry. You may feel hard-pressed on every side, but you will never be struck down by God's strength and care. The stresses of the world may leave you perplexed, but there is no need to despair. Yes, God is in control.

Philippians 4:6-7 is one of my favorite Bible verses. I quote this a lot as I deal with stress in life, and I would never be so cold-hearted as just to give someone a Bible verse if they are fighting anxiety and say, "good luck." However, I would talk about what Paul encouraged us, for those truths contain hope.

When Paul said to not be anxious about anything, He did not state that anxiety is a sin, but there is a better way. Constant worry will not help us in our situations. If we live in worry and never choose to believe that God can help us, that certainly can lead to sin. When we find ourselves paralyzed in fear, we can delight in Jesus and find peace even in anxiety. And we can do this in everything!

Keep talking to God! In *Suffering*, Paul David Tripp agreed that God will bring things into our lives that confuse us, and "at times we struggle to reconcile what God has said with what He's done. Sometimes God's declaration of who He is seems to contradict what He has ordained." (163) We find ourselves at a loss in proclaiming God's goodness and promises, yet experiencing debilitating challenges. As Paul stated, in everything, by prayer and supplication, he wants us to keep going to Jesus. You may not immediately feel better. Keep going to Him and trusting Him. Talk with a trusted friend, pastor, or counselor if needed. But all the while, in everything, trust that God is bigger than the anxieties you face. Do you know why? Because He is!

And then, begin to name all the things for which to be thankful, starting with Jesus. In despair, we can lose sight of the blessings of God. If you look hard enough, the blessings are there. When you look, you will see God, His fingerprints, His watch care, His providence, and His daily gifts. As you are persistent, something takes place. The peace of God, which is beyond anything you can think or understand, will protect your thinking and feeling. He will guard our hearts and minds in Him.

In the midst of our anxieties, we must acknowledge that God will never let us down. When Jesus died on the cross, He quoted Psalm 22:1 and said, "My God, my God, why have you forsaken me." I can't imagine how it must have felt when Jesus took our sin and the wrath of God.

Thankfully, I'll never have to do so. Jesus took what we deserved and felt forsaken by God so that we would never have to experience the same thing. Jesus felt the ultimate anxiety, so in our anxieties, we would know a Savior would forever be the peace of our lives. We should cast all our cares on Him, for He indeed cares for us.

No one compares to our God, and no power can overcome Him. He is in control, and my loving Father, who endured the cross, is right there with me every step of the way. He lives in us! Keep going to Him. He's got you, and He won't let go.

But they who wait for the LORD shall renew their strength; they shall mount up with wings like eagles; they shall run and not be weary; they shall walk and not faint (Isaiah 40:31).

- Ashley

REFERENCED VERSES

- Psalm 22
- Isaiah 40:31
- Matthew 27:46
- 2 Corinthians 5:21
- 1 Peter 5:7

FOR FURTHER STUDY

- *Spiritual Depression: Its Causes and Its Cure*, David Martyn Lloyd-Jones
- *Suffering: Gospel Hope When Life Doesn't Make Sense*, Paul David Tripp
- *The Emotions of God: Making Sense of a God Who Hates, Weeps, and Loves*, David T. Lamb
- *To Live Is Christ To Die Is Gain*, Matt Chandler

"BEAUTY FOR ASHES"

(1996)

Songwriter: Crystal Lewis

Artist: Crystal Lewis and Ron Kenoly

Album: *Beauty for Ashes*

Psalm 30:5–For his anger is but for a moment, and his favor is for a lifetime. Weeping may tarry for the night, but joy comes with the morning.

Isaiah 61:1-3–The Spirit of the Lord God is upon me, because the Lord has anointed me to bring good news to the poor; he has sent me to bind up the brokenhearted, to proclaim liberty to the captives, and the opening of the prison to those who are bound; to proclaim the year of the Lord's favor, and the day of vengeance of our God; to comfort all who mourn; to grant to those who mourn in Zion—to give them a beautiful headdress instead of ashes, the oil of gladness instead of mourning, the garment of praise instead of a faint spirit; that they may be called oaks of righteousness, the planting of the Lord, that he may be glorified.

90S IMPRESSION

God takes all of the bad stuff in our lives and makes good out of it.

TODAY'S IMPRESSION

God certainly takes the bad and works it all for good through His unfathomable sovereignty in His children's lives. Beyond that, He takes tragedies, grief, and hardship as they take place and sustains us by His strength and the peace of His presence.

What is the best trade you ever made? Maybe it involved a classic lunchroom trade you made back in the day, in which you upgraded what your mom packed and pawned off a healthy snack to some poor soul in exchange for their processed prize. Maybe you had a Ken Griffey, Jr., rookie card and got top dollar for it.

I remember a game we used to play in youth group called "Bigger Better." (You know, those infamous youth group games!) The game's premise was to give each team a penny, and they would have a couple of hours to trade up and come back to church with something better. I am amazed at the return people can get on a penny in a couple of hours. Groups come back with valuable sports jerseys and barbecue meals with all the fixings for the entire group, and one time someone actually got a car although I'm not sure if it ran.

The trades that God makes with us go beyond. We approach Him battered and torn, and offer our hurt and grief. We give Him our hardships, afflictions, and fears. What He gives us in return is bigger and better!

Funeral after funeral, I hear people say, "God won't put more on you than you can bear." I'm always respectful to them in their grief, but if I can lovingly guide them, I will say, "Actually, He *will* allow more on you than you can bear. He will, so we will put our trust in Him!"

The apostle Paul experienced affliction that was beyond what he could handle. He stated in 2 Corinthians 1:8 that he essentially wanted to die because things were so hard. Later, in 2 Corinthians 12, he said that God's strength is made perfect in our weakness (verse 9).

That's what God does. He takes our weakness and gives us His strength. He takes our desperation, and He comforts us with His loving presence. In our grief, Jesus is there taking care of us and experiencing every bit of what we endure. Since He is our life, He does that! We are weak and unable, and the all-powerful One comes and provides His divine, perfect strength!

To quote another late 90s worship song, we come to Him "Trading Our Sorrows!"

In Crystal Lewis's "Beauty for Ashes," she reminded us of this glorious truth. The song's timbre is soothing and soulful, matching the mood of the lyrics. Lewis, one of the top vocalists of 90s CCM, is joined by Ron Kenoly. Their duet lays a perfect foundation for meditating on this tremendous truth: God is taking what I am going through and giving me something better.

The lyrics come straight from the prophet Isaiah, and God's Word gives us insight into what the trade involves. God gives us something beautiful when we stand in a burnt heap. God takes our fears and replaces them with His strength. He takes our tears and mourning and brings us the gladness of knowing Him. And to be sure, this does not dismiss difficulty. Nor does it mean that all the struggles and grief cease entirely. It means we have at our disposal precisely what we need in hardship, and God is the only one who can provide it.

Isaiah 61 gives encouragement to those who are poor and broken-hearted. In the very beginning of the chapter, the prophet stated that the "Spirit of the Lord GOD is upon me" (verse 1). Isaiah was not talking about himself in this passage. Who is the anointed One who will bring good news to the poor and will bind up the brokenhearted? Who will open the doors to those who are bound?

Thankfully, Jesus makes it clear the passage is a messianic prophecy about Himself. I love when God puts the cookie on the bottom shelf for us! Jesus quotes this exact prophecy (See Luke 4:18-19.), which is about Him, when He began His ministry.

Therein lies the key to unlocking the trade deal we get. Jesus is the one who will comfort the mourning. Indeed, Jesus is the one who will take our ashes and make something beautiful. Jesus trades our fears for the peace of His presence! Sorrow may surround us, but Jesus is the Bigger and Better trade!

People seek to trade sorrows for other things in life. Those things might distract us or even make us feel better for a while. Some of the things are gifts from God. They are not all bad, but Jesus is bigger and better! He is the best! His trades pierce the core of our very being with His loving presence.

As I write this devotion, I recall a story that has been told many times in my family. There was a lot of fear when my mother was pregnant with my little sister. The fear stemmed from previously lost pregnancies and the reluctance to embrace the unknown and trust in the Lord. During this time, my mom found one of her life verses in Psalm 30. The psalmist said that "weeping may tarry for the night, but joy comes with the morning" (verse 5).

That is precisely what took place! After a long night of labor, my sister came into the world, and on an early morning, rejoicing became reality as April Joy was born! Yes, my mama gave my sister the name "Joy" as a reminder of God's faithfulness!

God is always working in ways we can't see, and His divine work is perfect. We put our trust in a loving and benevolent God who knows what is best and will always give us what is needed. In his classic *Morning by Morning,* Charles Spurgeon reminded us of this glorious truth.

> Every event as yet has worked out the most divinely blessed results; and so, believing that God rules all, that He governs wisely, that He brings good out of evil, the believer's heart is

assured, and he is enabled calmly to meet each trial as it comes. (August 6)

I know that every situation we endure, whether in grief or fear, doesn't have the exact ending we prefer, as in the birth of my sister. It might and it might not. Here is what I do know: God takes what we are going through and always gives us blessings. Jesus always knows exactly what we need. In our despair, we need Him.

- Ashley

REFERENCED VERSES

- Psalm 30:5
- Isaiah 61:1-3
- Luke 4:18-19
- Romans 8:28
- 2 Corinthians 1:8; 12:8-10

FOR FURTHER STUDY

- *Between Heaven and the Real World: My Story,* Steven Curtis Chapman with Ken Abraham
- *Choosing to SEE—A Journey of Struggle and Hope,* Mary Beth Chapman with Ellen Vaughn
- *Morning by Morning,* Charles H. Spurgeon (*https://www.heart-light.org/spurgeon/0805-am.html*)

"WE BELIEVE IN GOD"

(1993)

Songwriters: Amy Grant and Wes King

Artist: Amy Grant

Album: *Songs from the Loft*

> **2 Corinthians 5:17**–Therefore, if anyone is in Christ, he is a new creation. The old has passed away; behold, the new has come.

> **1 John 3:1-2**–See what kind of love the Father has given to us, that we should be called children of God; and so we are. The reason why the world does not know us is that it did not know him. Beloved, we are God's children now, and what we will be has not yet appeared; but we know that when he appears we shall be like him, because we shall see him as he is.

90S IMPRESSION

I believe in God!

TODAY'S IMPRESSION

I need a Savior, and finding myself in Jesus dictates who I am and who I become. I need to be rescued from my own desires and find peace in Jesus as He walks with me through life and defines who I am.

In 1993, a worship album featuring various artists hit the airwaves and poured out into Wednesday-night youth group gatherings across the country. *Songs from the Loft* began in the loft of a barn with a group of students, and it wasn't the barn where Steven Curtis Chapman was saddling up his horses. The loft was on the farm of Amy Grant, and the album featured many go-to artists of the 90s, including Smitty, Susan Ashton, Kim Hill, and Wes King, among others.

The album's genesis was a dream that Amy Grant and Gary Chapman had to fill the top of their barn weekly with students and talk to them about Jesus, study the Bible, fellowship, and, of course, sing. Several of the songs they sang made up this compilation featuring various artists with some kum-bah-yah-loving students, and it won the Dove Award for Worship Album of the Year in 1994. Many of the magnificent melodies will get you worshiping and having joy down in your heart (clap clap), down in your heart (clap clap), down in your heart to stay! (If you know, you know!)

"We Believe in God" may have been the most prominent radio hit on the record and seems to be getting back to the "Basics of Life" (Sorry, it is hard to resist the 90s puns!), but in reality, "We Believe in God" reveals the heart of the gospel. The song proclaims that we all need Jesus, and our need for Jesus is foundational in Christian identity.

Christians should constantly remind themselves of who we are in Christ and our need for Him. I've heard it said to "preach the gospel everywhere you go. And keep preaching it to yourself!" Realizing our need for a Savior and finding who we are in Him will provide peace and an anchor in a challenging landscape of a culture that often pulls away from what God desires. Identity in Christ leads to peace and assurance. When we put our identity in anything besides Christ, we struggle to find rest.

I believe that one of the biggest culprits in this battle is the fact that Christians have forgotten who they are! The worst case of identity theft is not someone hacking your social media profile or getting your Social Security Number. A tragedy takes place when the world seeks to derail a believer's biblical identity in who they are in Christ and replace it with falsehoods. As we proclaim that "We Believe in God" and need Jesus, we ultimately imply something that should guide us in our lives and witness.

Even more so, many Christians have forgotten whose they are! Paul's words in 2 Corinthians 5:17 in which he spoke of Christians being *new creations* are getting lost in the callings of the world. These cultural voices plead for us to find "our true selves" in things other than Jesus. By contrast, Christians find hope and identity in the miraculous truth that Christ now lives in us, and He is our very life.

When we realize Jesus is our very life, it will impact how we perceive our true selves. The God of all creation is our guide, and His Holy Spirit and the Word of God provide the direction we need. Our culture changes at light speed, yet God's Word remains true.

The battleground in this crisis is fragile self-esteem and doubts. It's scary that people seek peace in anything other than Jesus and feel it is their right to be individuals even if their search contradicts God's standards. If we are Christ's and realize He knows what is best for us, how wrong is that idea?

We must determine who will be our guide: the voices of the world or our heavenly Father?

Jesus died and rose again to give us peace that passes understanding! Our self-esteem should be grounded in the gospel and the work of Christ on the cross! Jesus loves extravagantly and lives in believers, so they do not have to live life playing the comparison game while striving for acceptance. The gospel is the remedy!

If you have accepted Jesus Christ by faith, you do not have to let others and their ideas control your thoughts. A biblical self-esteem and new identity in Jesus Christ reminds us that we belong because we are part of God's family (See Psalm 100:3.). What makes us important is who owns us. We are in the heavenly Father's family (See John 1:12.), and according to the apostle Paul, we will always be a part of God's family (See Romans 8:37-39.).

The opinion of others or the number of Facebook likes we get should not dictate our sense of belonging. Finding a group of friends that accept us in a "different lifestyle" will not bring sustaining peace. That is the job of the gospel!

Furthermore, we are worth something because, as the old saying goes, "God don't make no junk!" According to John 3:16, you are worth what Jesus did for you on the cross. God so loved you that His Son died for you (See Romans 5:8.). Think of the price that Jesus paid. We are worth an extravagant amount! If you are struggling and battling self-worth, find your worth in Jesus.

In *Gay Girl, Good God,* Jackie Hill Perry dealt with this issue. We must find who we are in God and allow that to be our foundation. Perry stated, "Christ has come to make us right with God. He is satisfying us in God." (190) When she became a new creation in Christ and realized that faith in God would not lead her astray, the simplicity of taking God at His Word became more important than the way she felt. And through faith, God moves us beyond our flesh, and we are satisfied with who we are in Him. He died on the cross so we would find our worth in His sacrifice and not ourselves.

Lastly, our confidence should not be in what the world thinks or even what we can do in our own strength. Competence comes when we know that whether hungry or full, clothed or naked, we will move forward in the strength of Jesus (See Philippians 4:13.). Inside every believer resides the Holy Spirit (See 1 Corinthians 3:16.), and nothing should encourage us more than to know God Himself lives inside us. My confidence is not in what I want to be, but in the strength of Christ in me.

The truth is that people really just want to be happy. In his famous work *Confessions,* Saint Augustine reminds us, "The happy life is joy based on the truth. This the joy grounded in you, O God, who are the truth, 'my illumination, the salvation of my face, my God'" (Psalms 2:6; 41:21).

As the song states, life is hard. It really is, and it might not get easier. Seek Jesus above all things, and He will never lead you astray. Keep reminding yourself of how much you need Him and who you are in Him, and don't be afraid to show it . . .

- Ashley

REFERENCED VERSES

- Psalm 100:3
- John 1:12
- Romans 5:8; 8:37-39
- 1 Corinthians 3:16
- 2 Corinthians 5:17
- Philippians 4:13
- 1 John 3:1-2

FOR FURTHER STUDY

- *Confessions of St. Augustine,* St. Augustine (*https://www.gutenberg.org/ebooks/3296*)
- *Crazy Love: Overwhelmed by a Relentless God,* Francis Chan
- *Gay Girl, Good God: The Story of Who I Was, and Who God Has Always Been,* Jackie Hill Perry
- *Identity: Who You Are in Christ,* Eric Geiger
- *The Pleasures of God: Meditations on God's Delight in Being God,* John Piper

"HOPE TO CARRY ON"

(1997)

Songwriter: Rich Mullins

Artist: Caedmon's Call

Album: *Caedmon's Call*

Romans 5:1-5–Therefore, since we have been justified by faith, we have peace with God through our Lord Jesus Christ. Through him we have also obtained access by faith into this grace in which we stand, and we rejoice in hope of the glory of God. Not only that, but we rejoice in our sufferings, knowing that suffering produces endurance, and endurance produces character, and character produces hope, and hope does not put us to shame, because God's love has been poured into our hearts through the Holy Spirit who has been given to us.

1 Peter 1:3-9–Blessed be the God and Father of our Lord Jesus Christ! According to his great mercy, he has caused us to be born again to a living hope through the resurrection of Jesus Christ from the dead, to an inheritance that is imperishable, undefiled, and unfading, kept in heaven for you, who by God's power are being guarded through faith for a salvation ready to be revealed in the last time. In this you rejoice, though now for a little while, if necessary, you have been grieved by various trials, so that the tested genuineness of your faith—more precious than gold that perishes though it is tested by fire—may be found to result in praise and glory and honor at the revelation of Jesus Christ. Though you have not seen him, you love him. Though you do not now see him, you believe in him and rejoice with joy that is inexpressible and filled with glory, obtaining the outcome of your faith, the salvation of your souls.

90S IMPRESSION

Since Jesus is God, He is my only hope for making it through this life.

TODAY'S IMPRESSION

Not only is Jesus God, but He is alive and lives in me. I have living hope through the love of my Savior who overcame the grave.

When Caedmon's Call hit the scene in the latter half of the 90s, they were a great addition to the musical landscape that was taking place in CCM! An earthquake of epic proportions took place in 1995 with dc Talk's *Jesus Freak,* followed by mammoth records from Jars of Clay and Audio Adrenaline, among others. Caedmon's Call found their own niche by combining a great deal of the late 90s sounds with a unique flair.

The band brought somewhat of a folk sound with an alternative rock vibe and would drive it home with lots of djembe drum! I loved it, and for several years they were my go-to! Their albums had so many great songs that rang out with theological depth. As a young seminarian, I was all about the theology the songs contained!

"Hope to Carry On" is a Caedmon's Call classic that brings to light an essential Christian doctrine with multiple layers one can pull back: Hope! The song is a cover of an older Rich Mullins song, and the late Ragamuffin artist is the writer. If you look up the retro video, Rich even makes a cameo appearance!

From the first listen, "Hope to Carry On" seems more simplistic in its message. But look deeper! As you look, ask yourself, "What is true hope, and is it guaranteed?" The answers to those questions get to the depth we find.

Christians misunderstand hope, and it often becomes a rolling-of-the-dice guessing game. We tend to say words like, "I hope so." When we say that, we are holding out or guessing that things will turn out OK. Conversely, hope in Jesus Christ is not "I hope so" and is no mere guessing game. If our hope is in Him, it is living hope!

In the opening remarks of 1 Peter 1, the apostle laid out the significance of the hope in which we live. The depth of our living hope leaps off the pages of Scripture!

Hope begins in Jesus and is a product of His mercy. In that mercy, He causes us to be born again. We were dead in our sins and trespasses, and are now alive in Jesus Christ! By the power of the Holy Spirit, He regenerates our hearts and comes to reside in us. What is the result of this new birth? Living hope!

Verse 3 of the passage links these ideas together. We are "born again into a living hope through the resurrection of Jesus Christ from the dead." Jesus is alive! If our hope is in the King of Kings and Lord of Lords who is alive, then it is a "living hope!"

If Jesus did not rise again, we would be back to the guessing game. We would be back to "I hope so." Our hope would be like any other religious person's hope in their religious holy man or founder. We would be guessing, wondering, and maybe even believing. Yet, our hope would be in someone still lying in a grave somewhere. However, Jesus overcame death by giving us resurrected hope because the Son that saved us is alive forevermore!

And what are the attributes of this living hope? Verses 4 and 5 paint a beautiful picture. It is "an inheritance that is imperishable, undefiled, and unfading, kept in heaven for you, who by God's power are being guarded through faith for a salvation ready to be revealed in the last time." This all takes place when we have faith and put our hope in Him.

Then Peter explained the reason why we need a living hope. We will endure grief in various trials and will experience a testing of our faith. As problems come, are we saying, "I hope I'm going to be OK," or are we placing our faith in Jesus, our living hope? Time will tell.

When our hope rests in our Savior, who is alive, we will find the hope to carry on. Another passage with similar theological insights is Romans 5. At the beginning of the chapter, Paul first mentioned our justification. We have discussed the idea of justification in other devotions, and realizing that we are declared righteous through our faith in Christ is mind-blowing. Being justified by Jesus is also the place to find living hope.

As we stand in His grace, we rejoice in hope. Then Paul got fatalistic. Well, actually, he didn't, but people are often confused by his statement. We are to rejoice in our sufferings, and that doesn't sound good! Am I supposed to be happy when bad stuff happens? That was not Paul's intention.

Living in a fallen world, no doubt we will experience suffering. Rejoice doesn't mean we are happy about the bad stuff. When you think about it, based on the word's etymology, rejoice means returning to the source of our joy. "*Re*" means "to go back," while "*joice*" is, of course, "joy." The only joy we have is in Jesus; no circumstance can take it away. In your suffering, always keep going back to Him.

A progression then takes place, and what a progression it is! As you continue to carry everything to Jesus, the reality, Paul stated, is that "suffering produces endurance, and endurance produces character, and character produces hope, and hope does not put us to shame, because God's love has been poured into our hearts through the Holy Spirit who has been given to us" (See Romans 5:3-5.). Look at what is taking place. God works in our sufferings as we find joy in Him; He produces inner endurance through His strength. We grow in character as we trust in His righteousness, and our trust in Him ultimately springs forth hope.

Our hope is attached to the Holy Spirit, Almighty God, living in us. And yes, it is a living hope because Jesus is alive, and it is hope that carries us onward!

Paul's words in 2 Corinthians 2:14 remind us where we are headed: "But thanks be to God, who in Christ always leads us in triumphal procession." As Dr. Lee Turner described:

> "Like fans that cheer and tear down the goal posts, we can joyously follow in His triumphal procession and daily participate in His victory." Jesus is victorious! So it only makes sense that He will lead us in victory, ultimately bringing Him glory, as we put our hope in Him. (*Discover Your Riches in Christ*, 25)

When we see Jesus on the cross, we see where our hope lies. When we know that we have been justified by faith and forgiven by Jesus, we understand that this is more than just rolling the dice.

Seeing that God makes a poor beggar rich and brings Peter to the place where he can put away his sword and no longer has to fight, we understand the gracious power of the hope that now lives in us. Love comes and brings us this hope. And it is all found in the overwhelming love of our Savior.

Because Jesus is alive, our hope in Him is a living hope that will never put us to shame. In Him is the only place to find hope to carry on!

- Ashley

REFERENCED VERSES

- Romans 5:1-5
- 2 Corinthians 2:14

- 1 Peter 1:3-9

FOR FURTHER STUDY

- *Discover Your Riches in Christ: They Are Out of This World!* Lee C. Turner
- *The Hand of God: Finding His Care in All Circumstances*, Allistair Begg
- *The Overcoming Life*, D. L. Moody

LIZ HUMOR

©LizKing

THEOLOGY OF PRAYER:

GET DOWN.

CHUMS MEET AMY GRANT

During the 90s at Austin Peay State University (APSU) in Clarksville, Tennessee (Let's Go Peay!), I was a privileged member of a secret fraternal organization. This group, though not a real fraternity, was intended to be a "mock" fraternity. Satire. Just to be clear, the society of brothers basically mimicked and ridiculed many of the things that my Christian college buddies and I loathed about fraternities.

Before anyone gets offended (not too hard these days), I'm not saying that all fraternities are of Satan. Many enter the Greek life and come away with lifelong friends and brothers, while also getting that "resume" info, and having a good experience. Some of my greatest Christian friends, who were very involved in fraternities, found lasting friendships and continually witnessed for Christ. Some just paid for friends and got drunk.

Conversely, my compadres and I thought frats were kind of silly, so we invented our own ridiculous group. We just didn't have to pay membership fees! This group was equipped with many sacred rites and rituals, many of which took place at the APSU Baptist Student Union prayer room. I could share some of them here, but then I'd have to, well, you know . . .

This group is famously known in those parts as the "Chums." Prerequisites to join were (1) having been on a mission trip, (2) able to quote Monty Python and the Holy Grail, (3) having been asked to be a Chum, and (4) being someone who has very chummy qualities. As silly and fake as it all was, it was kind of real, and other students actually did desire membership into this nonsensical devout brotherhood. One of my good buddies at the BSU desired membership, so we gave him a multi-page application to complete. We had decided that we weren't letting him in. After we received his application, we just stamped a big "Denied" on it, and delivered it to his campus P.O. box. To this day we still refer to him as "Gargamel, the eternal Black Ball." If I'm honest, I'm probably closer to my friend Troy (aka Gargamel) than any of the other Chums, but it was all just part of the revelry.

Once you graduated from college, you were a Chum-Alum. We even had a Chum princess, a grad student named Esther! Our mentor was the BSU director with the title, "Yoda, the Grand Mentor, and friend of chums." But I digress . . .

At this point you may be thinking, "What does this stroll down memory lane have to do with 90s CCM?" I'm glad you asked! You see, the Chums would often take road trips to various places. On one of these eventful road trips, we attended a Belmont University basketball game to cheer on one of my best friends. Many Nashville music celebrities frequented these games. The most popular would inevitably be Vince Gill. But quite often, you could sit right behind one Amy Grant and cheer on the "Rebels." (Mascot name has since been changed to the Bruins.)

One night the Chums devised a plan! We needed a picture with Amy Grant! She probably wasn't as popular as she was in the 80s, but she was still on the Mt. Rushmore of CCM. Who are we kidding? She's the queen! Undoubtedly, we had our "Hopes Set High." If we could get a picture with her, it would go down in the annals of time, and the photo could forever be hung on sacred walls for all to see. Maybe we might even be invited to her barn loft to sing worship songs!

Amy Grant is quite pretty and never seems to age. Of course, it wouldn't take much to make us look good! I was not able to attend the Million Man Promise Keeper March in Washington, DC, so I needed some things in my life to brag about. My young ego needed some important badges of 90s Christian manhood to add to my stonewashed jean jacket, which was pretty rad in the 80s!

As a 22-year-old in the 90s, Rebecca St. James might have had more street cred, but Amy Grant was no one's leftovers!

In typical chicken Chum fashion, we didn't ask Amy Grant for a picture. However, a friend of hers, who was in attendance at the game, saw us talking and politely asked, "Would you guys like a picture?" "Why, yes, we would!" "Every Heartbeat" was going full throttle that night, and today I have the Polaroid to prove it!

No doubt, Amy Grant is a pioneer of CCM. Anyone who can begin a career in the late 70s, influence the entire genre, and is still going, deserves our respect.

I know, I know. What about the whole "crossover" thing? Did she really sell out to demonic forces of the secular world to sell records? Is singing love songs a bad thing? Well, I'll have you know that "Baby Baby" was actually written about her 6-week-old baby for the "Heart in Motion" album. And I happen to call my wife "Baby," so I'm good with it!

- Ashley

"JESUS WILL STILL BE THERE"

(1993)

Songwriters: John R. Mandeville and Robert Matthew Sterling

Artist: Point of Grace

Album: *Point of Grace*

Psalm 23–The LORD is my shepherd; I shall not want. He makes me lie down in green pastures. He leads me beside still waters. He restores my soul. He leads me in paths of righteousness for his name"s sake. Even though I walk through the valley of the shadow of death, I will fear no evil, for you are with me; your rod and your staff, they comfort me. You prepare a table before me in the presence of my enemies; you anoint my head with oil; my cup overflows. Surely goodness and mercy shall follow me all the days of my life, and I shall dwell in the house of the LORD forever.

John 10:14-16–I am the good shepherd. I know my own and my own know me, just as the Father knows me and I know the Father; and I lay down my life for the sheep. And I have other sheep that are not of this fold. I must bring them also, and they will listen to my voice. So there will be one flock, one shepherd.

90S IMPRESSION

Jesus is always with me.

TODAY'S IMPRESSION

From our daily lives to the entire course of human history, God promises to be with us.

There's an amazing power in these two simple words: "I'm here." As a friend or a parent, it's probably the most meaningful words you could ever utter. Can you think of a time when those words were spoken to you and comforted you?

God has promised us that His Spirit is with us always, but sometimes grief and suffering can make it very hard to feel Him near. How can we be sure He is really there?

Elisabeth Elliot, missionary and wife of the late Jim Elliot, is a giant of the faith. She endured the tragic murder of her first husband, the passing of her second husband to cancer, and a decade-long battle with dementia in her later years. She was no stranger to suffering. Surely, this pain can cause any of us to doubt God's plan and even His good-ness. In *Suffering is Never for Nothing*, Elisabeth honestly ponders,

> So I would ask the question, is there a reason to believe that suffering is not for nothing? Is there an eternal and perfectly loving purpose behind it all? If there is, it's not obvious. It doesn't exactly meet the eye. Yet if for thousands of years in the face of these stunning realities–this terrible truth–people have believed that there is a loving God and that God is looking

down on the realities around us and still loves us. If these people have still continued to insist that God knows what He's doing, that He's got the whole world in His hands, then I repeat, the reason cannot possibly be obvious. It can't be because those thousands of people were all deaf, dumb, blind, or stupid and incapable of looking clearly and steadily at the data that you and I are constantly having to look at. What is the answer? (7)

Why, God? An intellectually honest person will ask and seek answers.

For Elisabeth, she resigned to the fact that most of us will never find a satisfying answer on this side of Heaven. But, she affirms, you can still find peace:

> The answer I say to you is not an explanation but a person, Jesus Christ my Lord and my God...He was giving me one unmistakable promise: I will be with you. For I am the Lord your God. He is the one who loved me and gave Himself for me. (12)

Have you ever felt the emotions described in "Jesus Will Still Be There"? Have you ever felt like you lost it all? Hope fading, you have no words to pray? Like a loving father to a child, He wants to soothe us in our grief. He does so, not with an intellectual answer that satisfies our curiosities, but with His presence. He is there. He is with you. His presence will be your peace.

From the beginning, it's always been God's desire to be close to His children. The whole counsel of Scripture reaffirms this overarching theme—God wants to be with us.

In the garden, He created Adam and Eve and made His home with them.

In our separation, He promised to send a Savior to bridge the great divide caused by our sin.

In the wilderness, He manifested as a cloud by day and a fire by night.

In the temple, He provided a temporary means to dwell with His people.

In our Immanuel, He sent "God with Us."

In His sacrifice, He conquered death with His resurrection, removing the separation caused by sin and death.

In His ascension, He assured us that we would never be alone, and He sent the Holy Spirit to reside in our hearts.

In the last days, when Jesus returns at last, He will unite us in whole and fellowship with us forever.

God created us to be with Him, and He desires to be with us forever. This is God's loving plan. Dying to reach you, Jesus proved that love with His own suffering, and He is the One who has made it possible to be with God once again.

A psalm that provides great comfort in times of distress is Psalm 23. A psalm of David, it describes the tender relationship of a shepherd who is dedicated to the care and comfort of his sheep. Even in the shadow of death, we can be confident that He is with us:

> Even though I walk through the valley of the shadow of death, I will fear no evil, for you are with me; your rod and your staff, they comfort me (verse 4).

How does the shepherd provide peace and comfort? With His presence. Calling us to Him, He leads us toward His house where we will dwell forever.

Psalm 23 means so much more to me when I consider how it fits within God's big picture to dwell with His people. He shepherds not only my life but the entire course of history to be with His flock. The past, present, and future are leading toward this goal. Since God has gone to such great lengths, He can surely be with us in our daily circumstances to comfort us.

Elisabeth Elliot shared how God used the suffering of losing her first husband, Jim, to bring her to greater knowledge of Him:

> Five days later, I knew that Jim was dead. And God's presence with me was not Jim's presence. That was a terrible fact. God's presence did not change the terrible fact that I was a widow and I expected to be a widow until I died because I thought it was a miracle I got married the first time. I couldn't imagine that I would ever get married a second time, let alone a third time. God's presence did not change the fact of my widowhood. Jim's absence thrust me, forced me, hurried me to God, my hope and only refuge.
>
> And I learned in that experience who God is. Who He is in a way that I could never have known otherwise. And so I can say to you that suffering is an irreplaceable medium through which I learned an indispensable truth. I Am. I am the Lord. In other words, that God is God. (15)

Suffering isn't wasted when we know He can use it to accomplish His great plan to bring us to Him and the fullness of His love. That's the whole truth.

If you ever have doubt, you aren't the only one. Some of the great heroes of the faith have doubted—Abraham, Peter, John the Baptist, and Thomas, to name a few. I feel as if doubters are in good company. Even still, Jesus promises to be there in the midst of the stormy waters of doubt, reaching out His hand to rescue us when we begin to sink. Will you allow Him to pull you back up? Will you follow where He leads? Elisabeth continued,

> Where does this idea of a loving God come from? It is not a deduction. It is not man so desperately wanting a god that he manufactures Him in his mind. It's He who was the Word before the foundation of the world, suffering as a lamb slain. And He has a lot up His sleeve that you and I haven't the

slightest about now. He's told us enough so that we know that suffering is never for nothing. (16)

Consider the whole big picture, from Genesis to Revelation. God has worked and is working to use all things for our good by bringing us into His presence. Amid life, love, and other mysteries, Jesus will still be there.

- Rachel

REFERENCED VERSES

- Psalm 23
- John 10:14-16

FOR FURTHER STUDY

- *God's Big Picture: Tracing the Storyline of the Bible*, Vaughan Roberts
- *Suffering is Never for Nothing*, Elisabeth Elliot
- *The Hiding Place*, Corrie Ten Boom
- *The House of Bondage: or Charlotte Brooks and Other Slaves*, Octavia V. Rogers Albert (*https://docsouth.unc.edu/neh/albert/albert.html*)

"AS IT IS IN HEAVEN"
(1995)

Songwriter: Michael W. Smith (from Matthew 6:9-13)

Artist: Michael W. Smith

Album: *I'll Lead You Home*

> **Matthew 6:5-13**–"When you pray, you must not be like the hypocrites. For they love to stand and pray in the synagogues and at the street corners, that they may be seen by others. Truly, I say to you, they have received their reward. But when you pray, go into your room and shut the door and pray to your Father who is in secret. And your Father who sees in secret will reward you.
>
> And when you pray, do not heap up empty phrases as the Gentiles do, for they think that they will be heard for their many words. Do not be like them, for your Father knows what you need before you ask him. Pray then like this:
>
> Our Father in heaven, hallowed be your name. Your kingdom come, your will be done, on earth as it is in heaven. Give us this day our daily bread, and forgive us our debts, as we also have

forgiven our debtors. And lead us not into temptation, but deliver us from evil.

90S IMPRESSION

This prayer includes all the checklist items to pray exactly the right way in order to please God. A magical formula exists that will bless any ballgame, sports team, wedding, or worship event when recited corporately.

TODAY'S IMPRESSION

Jesus ushers in a new kingdom, and the followers in that kingdom will begin to see God perhaps in ways they never had. The overwhelming idea that we pray to a true "Father" who radiates holiness and right-eousness as He sits on His throne and builds His kingdom is monu-mental. To be sure, our loving Father provides for His children's needs, both physically and spiritually.

Throughout my Christian upbringing, I often heard the traditional rendering of "The Lord's Prayer." The song wows at weddings, or perhaps your local church might have an ear-piercing soprano who brings the house down. I recall "the kingdom, and the power, and the glory, forever" reverberating through a red foam ice-cream cone micro-phone and crescendoing to the apex of the church rafters. A VHS tape may or may not exist where I am singing this version at my grand-mother's wedding during my early college years.

When Michael W. Smith chose to cut a new version of this traditional classic, I fully embraced it! The new melody was catchy and modern without disrespecting the original. An African choir, catchy drum beats, and an upsurging culmination made it inspiring. My wife and I even had it performed sign language-style for our wedding, which some people thought was enormously irreverent. The performance did not even contain any interpretive dance (aka Baptist dancing loophole)! Contemporary sign language in church? Serenity now! Some thought we shook things up a bit. When Jesus prayed this prayer, He did as well.

The timeless principles embodied within the Lord's Prayer bring a transforming perspective for New Testament believers. Dr. R. Albert Mohler, Jr., called it *The Prayer That Turns the World Upside Down*! Mohler suggested, "The primary theological foundation for prayer is the fact that there is one true and living God who has revealed Himself to us." (9) That raises the question: How has God revealed Himself to us in His model prayer?

To first understand how God has revealed Himself in the Lord's Prayer, we should notice how Jesus addresses God: "Our Father in Heaven" (Matthew 6:9). It's an interesting and seeming contradiction that the one all-powerful God who deserves all glory and praise would choose for us to come to Him as children to a loving Father. In Galatians 4:6, the apostle Paul stated, "And because you are sons, God has sent the Spirit of his Son into our hearts, crying, 'Abba! Father!'" Indeed, God is our Daddy!

A well-known piece of Jewish liturgy repeatedly describes God as "Avinu Malkeinu," our Father, our King. However, this idea of God as our Father as Jesus meant was revolutionary to many of Jesus' early followers. The Son ushered in grace which was ultimately demonstrated at the cross. A pious mindset ruled the day amongst religious rulers, and much about Jesus was revolutionary. Indeed, no one really knew His "Secret Ambition" was to make it possible for us to see and know God as Father in a new way! Jesus' prayer was not about being religious, but it was about knowing God intimately.

Second, in addition to God being the most magnificent loving Father of all, His very name is hallowed! Theologian R.C. Sproul put it this way: "The idea of holiness is so central to biblical teaching that it is said of God, 'Holy is his name'" (Luke 1:49). When we recognize who He is, what He has done, and that He is an immeasurable Holy Father, we have no choice but to fall to our knees and cry "Holy is Your name!" (*The Holiness of God*, 15)

The word "hallowed" means to "make it holy." When Jesus said, "Hallowed be your name," (Matthew 6:9), He not only stated the obvious but petitioned for God's name to be made holy on this earth just as it is in Heaven. In observing His holiness, we contemplate the incredible reality of a supremely divine, virtuous, and righteous God, who is to be recognized as such by His image bearers.

The rest of Jesus' prayer rests on this foundational request that God would demonstrate His holy and righteous will—on a cosmic scale all the way down to our daily bread. There is something so comforting about looking to our loving Father and saying, "Father, I need You. Make Yourself known here and bring about Your will."

There have been times when I have struggled with a situation or temptation in my life, and all I can pray is this simple prayer of surrender, "Hallowed be Your name." I've been so broken, so tired, so confused, and so ashamed, but this simple request completely encapsulates my desire to see God do what only He can do. Because I know my Father is loving, I know that His will is ultimately good and exactly what is needed.

Perhaps you, too, have been in a situation in which you don't know what to pray or how to pray. Whatever your struggle, pray that God's name will be made holy in your life. In times of joy, hallowed be His name. In times of trial, hallowed be His name. In times of temptation or defeat, hallowed be His name. May our prayers seek God's will, honor, and fame above all else.

Just a side note: You may be reading this and struggling with the concept of what a good father looks like, let alone a hallowed one. In fact, you may not even know your earthly father. But if you know Jesus and have trusted in Him, you have a Father above all fathers. Crawl up in His lap and allow Him to put His arms around you. Enjoy Him as He enjoys you. If you are a father or a parent, you know how much you love your children. Think about what you would do for them. Your heart's desire in all things is for your children to know how much you love them. How much more so do you think our Hallowed Heavenly Father loves His children? More than we can even imagine, praise God.

In summary, when we ask for God to show Himself to us and to be glorified in our situation, that changes our prayer life! We exalt Him because it rightly puts the focus where it needs to be. God is passionate about His glory illuminated in the world. As God, He deserves it! And beyond that, the hallowing of God's name is for our good! His desire to be glorified is not at odds with His desire for us to find joy in Him and know the beauty of His love and grace. When we find lasting joy in our Hallowed Father, we get the proper perspective in everything we bring before His feet.

- Ashley

REFERENCED VERSES

- Psalm 103:13
- Isaiah 6:3
- Luke 1:49
- John 17:11
- Galatians 4:6
- 1 John 3:1
- Revelation 4:8

FOR FURTHER STUDY

- *An Orthodox Catechism,* Hercules Collins
- *The Good News We Almost Forgot: Rediscovering the Gospel in a 16th Century Catechism,* Kevin DeYoung
- *The Holiness of God,* R.C. Sproul
- *The Lord and His Prayer,* N.T. Wright
- *The Prayer That Turns the World Upside Down: The Lord's Prayer as a Manifesto for Revolution,* R. Albert Mohler

"ON MY KNEES"

(1996)

Songwriters: David A. Mullen, Nicole C. Mullen, and Michael Hunter Ochs

Artist: Jaci Velasquez

Album: *Heavenly Place*

> **John 14:13-14**–"Whatever you ask in my name, this I will do, that the Father may be glorified in the Son. If you ask me anything in my name, I will do it."

> **1 John 5:14-15**–This is the confidence that we have toward Him, that if we ask anything according to his will he hears us. And if we know that he hears us in whatever we ask, we know that we have the requests that we have asked of Him.

90S IMPRESSION

Prayer is a powerful thing that changes me and the world around me.

TODAY'S IMPRESSION

Prayer is powerful when we pray in Jesus' name. When we do, we align our prayers and desires with His kingdom mission to glorify God. No matter how God chooses to answer our specific requests, we can trust that God's ultimate glory will be fulfilled.

Prayer is such a mystery to me. The idea that the Almighty God of the universe allows and even desires for us to have a conversation with Him is astounding. We have one-on-one access to an omnipotent Father who can move mountains!

Furthermore, Jesus said that "Whatever you ask in my name, this I will do, that the Father may be glorified in the Son. If you ask me anything in my name, I will do it" (John 14:13-14). Like you, Jaci, I'm not entirely sure how it works, but there is undoubtedly power when we humbly get on our knees in prayer.

One of the many blessings of being a believer in the body of Christ is witnessing when God answers specific prayers. We know that nothing is too hard for our God (See Jeremiah 32:27.)! However, I'm sure you can think of your own specific prayers that seem to go unanswered. Why is our child suffering in this way? Why did our loved one not receive healing? Why do evil and injustice continue to exist? Jesus, what did You mean when You said that we could ask anything in Your name and You would do it?

It hurts when God chooses not to answer our prayers in the way we hope. Jesus knows what that feels like. In the hours before His arrest, Jesus sweated blood and poured everything He had into intense prayer to His Father. At one point, Jesus fell on His face and pleaded, "My Father, if it be possible, let this cup pass from me" (Matthew 26:39). Jesus asked for God to find another way and to spare Him from the pain He was about to endure. God didn't answer that prayer, but

He did answer what Jesus prayed next, "Nevertheless, not as I will, but as you will" (verse 39).

Paul also had an unanswered prayer. He had his own "thorn … in the flesh" that he repeatedly asked God to take away (2 Corinthians 12:7-8). God chose to allow the thorn to stay, whatever it was. He had a plan and purpose for it that He would use for His glory. This thorn caused Paul to be weak so that He had to depend upon the power of Christ.

In perfect love and submission to God, Jesus always kept pursuing the fulfillment of God's glory even when everyone around Him didn't quite understand the bigger picture. To pray in Jesus' name means to pray in agreement with what Jesus prayed, and Jesus always prayed for God's kingdom, will, and glory to be revealed on Earth as it is in Heaven.

By looking at these "unanswered prayers" of Jesus and Paul, we get a small window into God's decision-making. Both prayers have something in common: God chose to respond in a way that would bring about His glory. God answers these prayers every time.

While we absolutely have power in Jesus' name, the power is to bring about God's glory. As we pray in Jesus' name, we reorient ourselves to align with Jesus' mission and desire to bring about His kingdom and glory on Earth. Our prayers become a means of participation in this cosmic plan ushered in by Jesus' death and resurrection (See 1 John 5:14-15.).

Praying in Jesus' name is an act of surrender and confidence in Jesus' ultimate mission and kingship. If I pray in His name, I'm not praying in my own. As Jesus did, we are free to make our requests known to God, nevertheless, we pray for God's will to be done above all. For ourselves, prayer in Jesus' name leads us toward loving obedience to our Father.

As we meditate on God's Word and see God's Spirit transform our hearts into Jesus more and more, our desires will begin to look like those of Jesus (See Psalm 37:4.). This intimate communion of shared desires between

God and us is a majestic and beautiful spiritual connection made possible through His Spirit. If you are seeking powerful prayers, ask the Holy Spirit to make Himself known to you in His Word and in your heart.

In his 1916 work *The Soul of Prayer*, Theologian P.T. Forsyth described how the Spirit changes our prayers:

> We can offer God nothing so great and effective as our obedient acceptance of the mind and purpose and work of Christ. It is not easy. It is harder than any idealism. But then it is very mighty. And it is a power that grows by exercise. At first it groans, at last it glides. And it comes to this, that, as there are thoughts that seem to think themselves in us, so there are prayers that pray themselves in us. And, as those are the best thoughts, these are the best prayers. For it is the Christ at prayer who lives in us, and we are conduits of the Eternal Intercession.

In other words, the Spirit makes us "conduits" for His will through prayer.

In our example of Paul, his prayer echoed the submission of Christ in that he wished for God's will above all else. As a result, God made Paul to be content with his "weaknesses, insults, hardships, persecutions, and calamities" (2 Corinthians 12:10). While Paul wasn't perfect, he is an example of what the Holy Spirit can do in and through us when we pray as Jesus prayed.

Indeed, prayer has great power to bring about God's glory in our lives and in the world. Mrs. Prudie, a faithful woman in our church, says, "I pray big things because I have a big God." Perhaps one day we will see the impact of our prayers in God's grand scheme. But, until then, whether on your knees, in a crowd, or by yourself, pray in His name in accordance with Jesus' purposes and trust that God will answer every time.

- Rachel

REFERENCED VERSES

- Psalm 37:4
- Jeremiah 32:27
- Matthew 26:39
- John 14:13-14
- 2 Corinthians 12:7-10
- 1 John 5:14-15

FOR FURTHER STUDY

- (For children) *Little Prayers for Ordinary Days,* Tish Harrison Warren, Katy Bowser Hutson, and Flo Paris Oakes
- *Prayer: Experiencing Awe and Intimacy with God,* Timothy Keller
- *The God I Don't Understand: Reflections on Tough Questions of Faith,* Christopher J.H. Wright
- *The Soul of Prayer,* P.T. Forsyth (*https://ccel.org/ccel/forsyth/prayer/prayer.iv.html*)
- (For children) *What Every Child Should Know About Prayer,* Nancy Guthrie

"WELL ALRIGHT"

(1994)

Songwriters: Keith Edward Crouch, John T. Smith, and CeCe Winans

Artist: CeCe Winans

Album: *Everlasting Love*

> **John 16:33**–I have said these things to you, that in me you may have peace. In the world you will have tribulation. But take heart; I have overcome the world.

> **Romans 8:28**–And we know that for those who love God all things work together for good, for those who are called according to his purpose.

90S IMPRESSION

God will make everything work out for the best.

TODAY'S IMPRESSION

God will make everything work out for the best, and you had better not forget it!

CeCe Winans has an unmistakable voice. She has the God-given ability to suck you into the emotion of every note she sings. Heaven help me when a CeCe song comes on when I'm alone in my mom van. As I belt along, she can count on me to be the Whitney for her duet. It's a good thing no one can hear me.

In her album *Everlasting Love*, the lyrics of "Well, Alright" speak directly to those who are hurting and desperately waiting for an end to suffering. With assurance and empathy, CeCe reminds her listeners that hope is within reach, a resolution to the pain is coming, and we can stand on God's promises. Therefore, although it doesn't feel like it, things will be alright. There's always hope.

Her words carry huge implications. We have a love, peace, and hope that all humans since the beginning of time have sought through every means imaginable. Not only does Jesus Christ freely give these undeserved gifts (See Ephesians 2:8-9.), but they will never be taken away from us (See Romans 8:35-39.). We actually do know that things will be alright in the end (See Romans 8:28.).

Be that as it may, for an everyday American Christian, this extraordinary news can sometimes feel rather ordinary as if we've heard this all before. If the spectacular has turned, dare I say, stale, what can we do about it?

In the 90s and still today, we love to slap Bible verses, like the ones mentioned above, on keychains, bookmarks, bracelets, and "pass it on" cards. Perhaps you have a mug with one of these standards in your cabinet right now: "Keep the faith," "Run the race," "Wait on the Lord," or "Be strong and courageous." But have you placed an "I Can

Do All Things Through Christ" Hobby Lobby print above the toilet? No? Well, that's just a missed opportunity right there.

Joking aside, it's not that we think any of those things are bad, but we can become desensitized. Unintentionally, we can morph these profound promises into mere superficial slogans, warm fuzzies, and meaningless Christianese. And that's not alright. Why? Because affliction is a guarantee in this fallen world. Jesus says we will suffer (See John 16:33.). When confronted with suffering and trials, flimsy feel-good emotions won't sustain us. And if that won't, what will?

CeCe reminded us to stand on God's promises like the one from Romans 8:28. However, if we have downgraded these truths to drive-by bumper stickerisms, we might wonder how to actually do that standing. How can we transform these familiar verses that we have heard over and over through the years from pretty platitudes to penetrating promises in our heart?

In his 1880 sermon "To Whom," preacher J.C. Ryle warned of a shallow Christian life,

> Let us never try to satisfy ourselves with a little cheap, formal Christianity, taken up carelessly on Sunday morning, and laid aside at night, but not influencing us during the week. Such Christianity will neither give us peace in life, nor hope in death, nor power to resist temptation, nor comfort in trouble. Christ only has "the words of eternal life," and His words must be received, believed, embraced, and made the meat and drink of our souls. A Christianity without living, felt communion with Him, without grasp of the benefits of His blood and intercession, a Christianity without Christ's sacrifice and Christ's Priesthood, is a powerless, wearisome form.

In other words, it's worth exploring how we can move into deeper belief. There's a lot we could be missing if we don't.

If anyone knew about cultivating faithfulness and deeper belief, it was perpetually persecuted Paul. What did he say to do? While in chains,

Paul gave the faithful Philippian church very practical counsel. He exhorted them to rejoice in the Lord, make requests known to God with thanksgiving, and meditate on what they learned. As they do this in obedience and gentleness, the peace of God will guard their hearts and minds through Christ Jesus (See Philippians 4:4-8.).

Is it really that uncomplicated? Yes! Mysteriously, God works through the plain simplicity of a rejoicing and thankful spirit communing with Him and a mind meditating on His Word. His Spirit brings about a transformation in our spirit. He is also our helper who teaches us and helps us remember (See John 14:26.). Moreover, when we serve and learn in community with unified fellow believers, the Spirit allows us to experience these spiritual blessings together.

His promises are the solid ground we need, and His Spirit can give us the legs to stand on them. If you experience pain and suffering and the promises of God seem superficial or old news, rest assured the Holy Spirit can change that for you. Experience the profound goodness of our God through thanksgiving, supplication, and meditation of His Word. Join together with other believers to serve and love. Be ready to follow where the Holy Spirit leads.

Finally, although you've probably read this numerous times, I've got one more promise for you. Look again with fresh eyes and be encouraged for what God will do in you for His glory: "And I am sure of this, that he who began a good work in you will bring it to completion at the day of Jesus Christ" (Philippians 1:6). Well, alright!

- Rachel

REFERENCED VERSES

- John 14:26; 16:33
- Romans 8:28; 8:35-39
- Ephesians 2:8-9
- Philippians 1:6; 4:4-8

FOR FURTHER STUDY

- *Praying the Bible, Donald S. Whitney*
- *Savoring Scripture: A Six-Step Guide to Studying the Bible,* Andrew Abernethy
- *The Way of Grace: Finding God on the Path of Surrender,* Glandion Carney with Marjean Brooks
- "To Whom," J.C. Ryle (*http://www.tracts.ukgo.com/ryle_to_whom.pdf*)
- *Word in Habit: How to Study and Apply the Word of God,* Cameron Frank and Preston Norman
- *Word in Heart: The Life-Changing Discipline of Scripture Memory,* Cameron Frank

LIZ HUMOR

Uncomfortable 90's Christian pick up lines..

Hey girl! I was readin' the book of Numbers and I realized I didn't have yours..

UGH!

Is your name Barbara? Because you're the one for me!!!

Hey girl! I got a big big house with lots of room. You wanna see it?

OOOHH WHEEE! You must be filled with the Holy Ghost girl, because YOU ARE ON FIRE!!!

I have the gift of tongues. Mind if I practice on you?

BTR

You're so fine I might sneak in your house and uncover your feet while you're sleeping...

You know the Bible says it's better to marry than burn with desire!

God told me you're the one I'm supposed to marry, you just don't know it yet!

BIBLE

The Bible says it's not good for man to be alone...

I AM NOT DESPERATE

©Liz King

THEOLOGY OF EVANGELISM:

GO LIGHT YOUR WORLD!

LIZ HUMOR

©Liz King

CHRISTIAN MUSIC WAS IN MY FUTURE

BY KEVIN MCNEESE, PRESIDENT AND FOUNDER OF
NEWRELEASETODAY.COM

I knew it immediately after performing a human video to Carman's "The Champion" on a summer mission trip to Guatemala at age 13. It was not because I killed my performance in the ring with the main character (which I did), but because afterward, during group prayer, one of the lead pastors traveling with us prayed over me and prophesied that I would be involved in "music ministry."

I didn't play an instrument. I didn't sing in the choir. I didn't listen to or care about Christian music. My cassette collection at the time consisted of Michael Jackson, Billy Joel, and Bruce Springsteen's *Born in the U.S.A.* (the first album played in my first Walkman). The 1997 track from Carman, who would later become a staple of my teenage years, was picked for us by our youth pastor, who told us to "act it out."

So, this vision spoken over me meant next to nothing. It was simply a nice random and encouraging message from an older woman I admired and respected. I thought nothing of it as my early teen years marched on.

Then, a few years later, I encountered Audio Adrenaline's *Don't Censor Me* (an album I wrote about in my previous retrospective), and everything started to click into place. Like every teenager before me, I was beginning to figure out what a relationship with God looked like in my life. This music spoke into that building curiosity in a way different from everything my parents, and most peers, were listening to.

My "Glory Days" were about to get a radical redefining, and my response to discovering Christian music was immediate and purposeful: Who else can I share this with?

As I dove deeper into the emerging world of Christian pop and rock, that desire to find anyone who would listen grew stronger. I guess that's what all music does. It's a form of entertainment designed to be sharable in community. The more, the merrier.

During my junior high and high school days, I looked for every opportunity to incorporate Christian music into my life and, without even realizing it, began to live out the calling God had brought to me at age 13.

I quickly amassed a large collection of Christian CDs by visiting local Christian bookstores every week, and spending hours listening to demos and thumbing through copies of *CCM* and *7Ball* magazines. I budgeted out months' worth of wish lists with the mail-order music subscription club Columbia House. With a massive collection in tow, I began hosting listening parties at youth groups and DJing local parties and skate nights at the roller rink. At the same time, I joined the youth choir, picked up the saxophone, and started playing in my church's worship band. Music ministry was becoming my life.

Before I knew it, my passion for introducing people to Christian music, born from a direct calling I wasn't fully aware of, reached a new level.

The music I listened to and was passionate about getting others to listen to didn't get played on the radio, which bothered me. The local contemporary station focused on older artists such Steven Curtis Chapman, Wayne Watson, and Kathy Troccoli. I was discovering, and listening to, dozens of incredible, life-changing albums from newer artists such as Plumb, Big Tent Revival, and Smalltown Poets, all of which were nowhere to be found on the air. I was becoming frustrated running into narrow perceptions of what Christian music offered, and it was time to do something about it.

After being turned down by the local contemporary station, a local Christian talk station offered me two hours every Saturday night to run my own music show. Why? No clue other than "God knows." I had no radio experience. I had no business experience. I was an 18-year-old young adult with a bunch of CDs and a lot of passion. Once I collected $500 a month for the airtime, I had a block of time to play whatever I wanted.

And so, I secured a few sponsors from generous business owners in my church happy to support a kid's dream, and I started a two-hour radio show called "The Rock." To say it was "amateur hour" would be an understatement. After a crash course in studio training, they turned me loose. *LIVE.* The analog system had me shuffling CDs, and sponsor ads were recorded on cartridges. I would accidentally fire off spots over songs. I would do entire breaks without turning the microphone on. I would play two songs at once, announce the wrong tracks, give out the wrong phone number, and do everything short of burning the studio down. But I was playing music that few people heard. And it was glorious.

I immediately discovered that I needed to own more music. Short of borrowing from friends and saving up every buck I could for the local Christian bookstore, it wasn't enough to keep a two-hour show fresh and current. There was just so much music coming out every month. I quickly struck up a deal with the local Christian bookstore. I would advertise for them for free every month in exchange for CDs.

Things were going great—until that night.

I had just received the new album, *The Hoodlum's Testimony*, from rapper T-Bone (1997) and was debuting his single "Demon Executor" on the show. About halfway through the song, I noticed the lights on the studio phone start to illuminate. I ignored it since no one had trained me to answer the phone.

Now, keep in mind that this was a station that played zero music. The programming before and after The Rock radio show consisted of nationally syndicated preaching–talk radio that was geared toward an audience four times my age. Apparently, they were not happy with the gang-banging, demon-hating rapper. They tuned in that night for some friendly Jesus preaching only to hear lyrics that promoted throat-slashing demons, banging together demon's heads like a tetherball, and using a sniper's scope to defeat a demon's hope. In hindsight, I should have used more discretion.

I received a call the next morning to meet with the station owner, and he was not happy. He gave me a few more weeks to wrap up my prepaid month, and that was that. The Rock ended its short, eight-month run.

While it was sad to see that dream die, God's plan for me was just getting started, and sharing Christian music with people in unique, wild, and crazy God-sized ways has remained a defining cornerstone in almost everything I've done since. This was before God opened an opportunity for me in Grand Rapids, Michigan, working for a dot-com start-up writing about Christian music. This was before I would spend five years being part of a pioneer team selling and marketing Christian music online when physical product was still the only way to consume music. And it was well before I would plant roots to begin a Christian music site that became *NewReleaseToday.com*, welcoming tens of millions of visitors throughout the past two decades and connecting them to what's new each week in Christian music.

Even though I learned many things along the way, seeing God's faithfulness in a promise He gave me back in 1991 drives me. We have to share Christian music because it contains the Gospel. It reaches struggling, hurting, disenfranchised, alone, hopeless, and forgotten people and reminds them that God is with them. Always. Nothing else matches music's universal language and power, so I share it wherever and however I can.

God knew I'd be passionate about His wonderful story and love for us through music. I will be listening and sharing as long as I have breath.

"SHINE"

(1994)

Songwriters: Steve Taylor and Peter Furler

Artist: Newsboys

Album: *Going Public*

> **Matthew 5:16**–In the same way, let your light shine before others, so that they may see your good works and give glory to your Father who is in heaven.

> **John 1:14**–And the Word became flesh and dwelt among us, and we have seen his glory, glory as of the only Son from the Father, full of grace and truth.

> **2 Corinthians 4:6**–For God, who said, "Let light shine out of darkness," has shone in our hearts to give the light of the knowledge of the glory of God in the face of Jesus Christ.

90S IMPRESSION

As Christians, we should let our light shine!

TODAY'S IMPRESSION

Christians should not only be lights for Jesus but stick out from the crowd because we are so different. The magnificence of the glory of God in our lives will be glaring to the lost world. As people see that glory and God works in Christians' hearts, they will want what we have!

In addition to being one of the most iconic CCM songs of the 90s, the Newsboys' "Shine" also had one of the most memorable videos. To say it was out there is an understatement. However, the creativity and individuality of 90s CCM is one more aspect of the decade that sets it apart.

I can see it now. A hamster wheel appears, and before you know it, an Asian geisha has eaten the poor hamster like a teen scarfing down pizza at a lock-in. Newsboys band members sing with heads harnessed in a contraption that looks like one of those eye air puffers everyone hates at the optometrist. (I honestly don't know what the contraption is, so if you read this and do, please email us!) Disco balls abound! And straitjackets. Strong men in tutus. A whole cast of strange characters doing some goofy dance. Eyeballs from the faces in the "eye puff torture mechanism" are twisting and turning.

As a CCM fan in the early 90s, I was a softy. My jam was Steven Curtis Chapman, 4HIM, and Michael W. Smith. To be completely honest, the video freaked me out. It was weird.

I just watched it again in preparation for writing this devotion. It is still weird. However, I see something that I didn't get in 1994. It is supposed to be weird. To a lost world, Christians can be weird. People thought Jesus was weird. The world will think the same of us. Yet in God's divine plan, His Spirit opens up the eyes of the lost to see what is different about us—Jesus.

The video contains an Easter egg that briefly flashes, telling us exactly where to go to learn more about this illumination. A white poster board displays Matthew 5:16, which is, "In the same way, let your light shine before others, so that they may see your good works and give glory to your Father who is in heaven."

Right in the heart of the Sermon on the Mount, Jesus tells His believers to shine! Why? To give glory to God.

Since the point of shining is to give glory to God, let's ask, "What is glory?"

Glory can become "Christianese." You know, that foreign tongue embedded in the Christian vernacular of which the lost world hasn't a clue of what we speak. When you approach an unbeliever and say, "You need to be sanctified by the blood of the Lamb and justified by faith," you may get a look like a cow staring at a new gate. It isn't that we are scared to share those ideas. Just don't be surprised if a lost world is confused by our churchy talk.

Much is the same with the idea of God's glory. To be honest, many Christians might also struggle to define God's glory. A reputable, scholarly theologian such as John Piper would define the glory of God as follows: "The glory of God is the infinite beauty and greatness of God's manifold perfections." God is perfect and divine and beautiful beyond imagination. You might say that God's glory is His holiness on display.

Essentially, God's glory is the beauty that shines from who He is. His glory is perfect, eternal, and divine. It is an outflow of who He is in all His glorious and majestic ways!

It's humbling to think that we as humans can take part in revealing God's divine glory. In fact, this is part of our vocation that we received back in Genesis when we were created to bear His image.

In *Why the Gospel?* Matthew Bates explained that our sin caused a glory deficit of sorts (See Romans 3:23.). When our ability to be the image of God became corrupted by sin, we became "lacking [in] the glory of God." (68) The good news of the gospel is that Jesus has come to restore that glory. Bates explained, "Proper image-bearing increases glory for humans, creation, and God." (63) For us, to shine is to allow the Spirit to mold us into the image of Jesus–the light of the world (See John 1.).

In John 1, Jesus' beloved disciple proclaimed that we have seen the glory of God in Jesus, the perfect image-bearer! This mention of glory is a reference to Old Testament passages that describe the manifestation of the presence of God. His glorious presence was manifested in places such as the Tabernacle or the temple. When Jesus arrived on the scene in the flesh, He tabernacled among us. His glory shone in the flesh, not merely in a holy place.

And through the blood of Christ, we become His tabernacle! We, too, manifest His glory. As partakers in His glory, who now house the very Spirit of God, His glory should shine in our lives. We daily live in Jesus, and He shines in us. If the glorious Spirit of Christ is shining through us, it will be a light that causes the world to take notice. As we live and love, through Christ, we shine! Indeed, it will be the kind of light that darkness cannot overcome!

The images in the video of "Shine" seem odd, yet the lyrics are poetic. If you bust out your old CD liner notes and spend some time reading the lyrics, you will be amazed by the symbolism and thought-provoking ideas. The verses can almost seem abstract and raw, much like the images in the video; then, the chorus brings the poetry alive.

We should look different. People should see that we enjoy being Christians and aren't bored with Jesus. There's nothing boring about God's magnificent glory. People should see something so glorious in us that they wonder how that could be us. The fact is, it's not us. It's Jesus. We are crucified with Him, and it is now His life we are living. People should look at us and perhaps think, "I think I'd like to have what he's having."

Shine.

- Ashley

REFERENCED VERSES

- Matthew 5:16
- John 1
- Romans 3:23
- 2 Corinthians 4:6

FOR FURTHER STUDY

- *A Peculiar Glory: How the Christian Scriptures Reveal Their Complete Truthfulness*, John Piper
- "Ask Pastor John: What is God's Glory?" *Desiring God* (*www.desiringgod.org/interviews/what-is-gods-glory--2*)
- *Evangelism Is...: How to Share Jesus with Passion and Confidence,* Dave Earley and David Wheeler
- *God's Greater Glory: The Exalted God of Scripture and the Christian Faith,* Bruce A. Ware
- *Lifestyle Evangelism: Crossing Traditional Boundaries to Reach the Unbelieving World,* Joe Aldrich
- *Why the Gospel?: Living the Good News of King Jesus with Purpose,* Matthew W. Bates

"TESTIFY TO LOVE"

(1997)

Songwriters: Paul Donald Field, Ralph Van Manen, Henk Pool, and Robert Tyrone Riekerk

Artist: Avalon

Album: *A Maze of Grace*

Psalm 121:1-2–I lift up my eyes to the hills. From where does my help come? My help comes from the LORD, who made heaven and earth.

John 9:25–He answered, "Whether he is a sinner I do not know. One thing I do know, that though I was blind, now I see."

Acts 1:8–"But you will receive power when the Holy Spirit has come upon you, and you will be my witnesses in Jerusalem and in all Judea and Samaria, and to the end of the earth."

90S IMPRESSION

To be a good witness, you need to be perfect.

TODAY'S IMPRESSION

As born again followers of Christ, we are witnesses when we allow others to see how Christ is living in and through our victories and failures.

This song hit during the WWJD craze. In case you aren't familiar, WWJD stands for "What Would Jesus Do." Bracelets with the abbreviation "W.W.J.D." were popular among Christians; the question was even the title of a hit CCM song by Big Tent Revival.

Certainly, nothing is inherently wrong with asking ourselves that important question. We should! Amid the popularity, the question carried along with it a sense of rule-based perfectionism. As a witnessing tool, the bracelet was a friendly reminder of how you should act so that others could see Jesus in your life. Doing what Jesus would do meant following all the rules, never making mistakes, and being perfect. In other words, if you wanted to bring others to Christ, you needed to be perfect like Jesus.

As misguided as that might be about the true intentions of WWJD, that was what my 90s teenage self got out of it. Relatively new in my faith, I was still figuring out what it meant to be a witness of Jesus. I knew I was supposed to "testify to love," but I wasn't sure what that meant. To answer that question, let us go back to Acts 1:8 where Jesus used that word "witness" to describe us.

In Acts 1:8, Jesus told his apostles to stay in Jerusalem so that they would receive power from the Holy Spirit. Jesus had established His kingdom on Earth and was sending out His born again followers as kingdom ambassadors into the world. Their task seemed straightforward: Be His witnesses through the power of the Holy Spirit. In the verse, Jesus was speaking to the apostles, but, since we share in one Spirit, we are His witnesses, too.

It wasn't until my freshman year of college in 1999 that my understanding of "witness" was turned upside down. My college professor at Toccoa Falls College was teaching on Acts 1:8. He told us that the word "witness" in that verse is the Greek word that we use for our English word "martyr."

Strong's Concordance defines witness and its Greek *martys* from Acts 1:8 to mean: "Those who after his example have proved the strength and genuineness of their faith in Christ by undergoing a violent death" and also "serve him by testimony." (Strongs NT 3144)

It's the connection to our word "martyr" that made me think. In Luke 14:27, Jesus said that we are to carry our cross. To the Jews of the day, they would have known exactly what Jesus meant by the word "cross." The Roman cross represented a gruesome, painful, and very public way to die. Jesus died that most violent death for our sins, and now our old sinful man must also die, too, in the same way. Our old selves died so that we could be born again into the life Jesus gives.

Living born again is a new way to be human—a total dependence on the power of the Holy Spirit rather than our own strength. Yet, being born again doesn't mean we don't have hardships. While we wait for the full redemption of our bodies, we struggle to be perfect as our heavenly Father is perfect (See Matthew 5:48.). That ongoing tug-of-war battle between our flesh and Spirit means that sometimes we win (when we lean on the power of His Spirit), and sometimes we lose (when we lean on our own power).

Losing can be humiliating, especially when we know others have seen us do the very opposite of what Jesus would do. In order to "protect" your witness of Jesus, have you ever hidden your less-than-perfect moments? Perhaps you think of your witness as a brand or PR campaign that you must cultivate like a social media page. Crop, edit, and rotate until you think your life is reflecting Jesus just right. Grab that fig leaf filter to cover up any mistakes!

Is protecting your image really what Jesus meant when He said, "Take up your cross," or "Be my witness"?

Herein lies the heart of the matter: Have you been born again? If so, you are a witness. You already are, just as you are, wherever you are—the good, the bad, and the ugly. Jesus didn't ask if you wanted to opt-in, complete a 90-day training course, or settle all your issues before becoming a witness. I believe He has a reason for that; our struggles are part of our witness as we take up our cross for all to see (See John 9:25.).

What does a dead-to-self witness look like? When you want to give up, testify to His faithfulness. When you sin, testify to His forgiveness. When you are tempted, testify to His goodness. When you are mourning, testify to His nearness. When you are anxious, testify to His peace. When you doubt, testify to His wisdom. When you are weak, testify to His strength. In everything, testify to His love.

If you want to show Jesus' perfect love to the world around you, show everyone how Jesus loves an imperfect person as yourself. Share your struggles and your pain so that you can share the source of your hope. "For when I am weak, then I am strong" (2 Corinthians 12:10).

Let me share with you the story of my friend. In her younger years, she made the very painful decision to have an abortion. After becoming a Christian, she kept her abortion a secret. Ashamed and embarrassed, she intellectually understood that God forgave her for all of her sins, but she remained in doubt that God would forgive her of that particular one.

After attending a confidential Bible study called "Surrendering the Secret," she realized that she had not been truly trusting in the power of the cross to give her total forgiveness. After that study, she began to cling to the truths of the gospel in a new and profound way. She now *knew* forgiveness.

Moved by the Holy Spirit, she began ministering to mothers and fathers on the sidewalk outside of a local abortion clinic. As she engaged with these abortion-minded parents, she retold and relived her pain in order to proclaim with conviction how God was the answer they were seeking.

My friend now leads "Surrendering the Secret" Bible studies for other post-abortive women. By experiencing God's love and forgiveness in her greatest struggle, she can personally testify to His glorious redemption and loving-kindness. If God has brought you through it, testify to it.

See, if you are a follower of Christ, you are a witness, too. You died and are made alive in Christ. As we remember our death, we know that God brings victory even in our moments of public and private defeat. Don't be afraid to share how God is working in your weakness and brokenness. For as long as we shall live, may we testify to love (See Psalm 121:1-2.).

- Rachel

REFERENCED VERSES

- Psalm 121:1-2
- Matthew 5:48
- Luke 14:27
- John 9:25
- Acts 1:8
- 2 Corinthians 12:10

FOR FURTHER STUDY

- *Real Life: A Christianity Worth Living Out*, James Choung
- *Messy Spirituality: God's Annoying Love for Imperfect People*, Mike Yaconelli
- If you are heartbroken from a past abortion, you are not alone. Find help at *surrenderingthesecret.com* or *saveone.org*.
- To begin an abortion sidewalk ministry in your church, contact *SpeakfortheUnborn.com*.

"LUV IS A VERB"

(1992)

Songwriters: George Cocchini, Mark Heimermann, and Toby McKeehan

Artist: dc Talk

Album: *Free at Last*

> **2 Corinthians 5:14-15**–For the love of Christ controls us, because we have concluded this: that one has died for all, therefore all have died; and he died for all, that those who live might no longer live for themselves but for him who for their sake died and was raised.

> **1 John 3:18**–Little children, let us not love in word or talk but in deed and in truth.

90S IMPRESSION

Love becomes a reality when an action takes place.

TODAY'S IMPRESSION

True agape love is supernatural, and it is a choice. That choice to love is foundational in all we strive to do as Christians. This love is possible because of God's love shown to us and implanted in our hearts.

Are you d- d- down with the dc Talk?

Now that we have the cheesiness out of the way, let's get to love! Before Smitty encouraged us to "give it away," the Decent Christian Talking boys were breaking it down and getting real.

Luv is a Verb.

If you are new to 90s CCM, that is not a typo. Sometimes you have to spice it up; changing the spelling of LOVE to LUV is fun and gets people's attention. Kind of like, "Ashley wuz here." You get the point.

The message remains true whether you spell it with a "U" or an "O." Love is something we do. Love isn't a mere feeling as is often proclaimed. And, love doesn't take place by sheer happenstance. Love is intentional and is a choice.

As Christians, people should know us by our love. We should exhibit love, walk in, move in, and trust in Jesus' love as we actively express love in what we do. The world should know we are Jesus' disciples in how we love one another! The greatest commandments of Jesus center on love (See Matthew 22:36-40.).

This love fest all sounds pretty elementary, right? Break out the marshmallows and kick off Kumbaya! Just as kindergarteners might accidentally misspell LUV, how can we mess this up?

Yet, we do. The song reminds us that love is a serious thing, and, yes, it's simple. When it works in the life of a believer as intended, the action verb of love is profound and life-changing. Thankfully, we can embark upon this kind of love because of its divine origin and how it shapes our lives.

We must first understand God Himself is the source of love. The well-known biblical idea of *agape* love is an excellent place to start.

Various ancient Greek words translate into the English word "love." *Phileo* is a friendship kind of love. Think "Philadelphia," the city of brotherly love. *Eros,* from which we derive the English word "erotic," is another type of love. This would be a more sensual kind of love. That doesn't mean it is bad if in the proper marital context, but it is not *agape.*

The love we speak of now is agape love. It is the highest form of love, God's love for man and the love of man for God. This love is not sappy or sentimental but profound and sacrificial. Agape love does not take action because it sees a lovable or admirable quality in its recipient. No, this kind of divine love takes effort because of its divine roots. God is love. He takes the first action in loving us when we were lost in sin. When we were dead in our trespasses, He loved us. He chooses to love us and show us His love in incredible ways (See John 3:16; 15:13; Romans 5:8; Ephesians 2:4-5; 1 John 3:1; 4:9-11.).

You see, not only is God the source, He is the example of love! We know what love is because we have seen its gracious benevolence. The gospel message is God's "show and tell" of love on display.

As His love implants in our hearts, He enables us to love the world around us with His kind of love. This verb of love is to take action in our lives among fellow believers, friends, enemies, and those we struggle to love. Even if we struggle or disagree with someone's choices or lifestyle, we should love. The people we are least likely to love may be the ones who need to see the love of God in action. Remember, often, people do not care how much you know until they know how much you care.

In 1 John 4:7-8, John encouraged us to love one another. And then the passage is clear that love is of God! If we are of God, we are to love because God is love!

Let's detour a little from 90s CCM into 80s pop. Remember when Tina Turner sang, "What's Love Got to Do With It?" When it comes to Christianity, the answer is everything.

We can overwhelm people with our vast theological knowledge and wow them with our spirituality. According to 1 Corinthians 13, your righteousness is about as practical as your VHS tape collection if you are not loving. Your supposed grandiose Christian walk and worship will seem irrelevant to someone if they are not experiencing the love of God through you. Again, this is not sappy or sentimental. To be sure, it is not turning a blind eye to sin. Agape love is an authentic action in humble, selfless works. This love is what Jesus did for us, and what we must do to others.

Yep, Luv is a verb.

When we look at Paul's exhortation in 2 Corinthians 5, we see Christ's love controls us, and other translations say "compels" us. As recipients of grace who contain the Spirit of Christ, we are moved to action by His loving Spirit within.

Not only is God the source and example of love, but He is also how we love.

In *Crazy Love*, Francis Chan discussed how love in action doesn't come naturally. We must pray for God to move us to love as we abide in Him and not give way to our selfishness. Christians must come to grips with the fact that we need the love of God to compel us to love.

Chan reminded us,

> Something mysterious, even supernatural must happen in order for genuine love for God to grow in our hearts. The Holy Spirit has to move in our lives. It is a remarkable cycle: Our prayers for more love result in love, which naturally causes us to pray more, which results in more love . . . (103-104)

In 1 John 3:18, John reminded us that talking about love is insufficient. We must live love and take action in love.

I absolutely luv Eugene Peterson's translation of 1 Corinthians 13:1-3 from *The Message*:

> If I speak with human eloquence and angelic ecstasy but don't love, I'm nothing but the creaking of a rusty gate. If I speak God's Word with power, revealing all his mysteries and making everything plain as day, and if I have faith that says to a mountain, "Jump," and it jumps, but I don't love, I'm nothing. If I give everything I own to the poor and even go to the stake to be burned as a martyr, but I don't love, I've gotten nowhere. So, no matter what I say, what I believe, and what I do, I'm bankrupt without love. (MSG)

We can do a lot of fantastic-looking, spiritual things. But, if we are not exemplifying love, none of it matters. As recipients of the love of God, Christians must exhibit His love. God's love at work in our lives should lead to action. Smitty was right. For love to be real, we must live it and give it away to others.

The love Jesus puts inside us must drive us to serve, to be better husbands and wives, as well as better parents and children. God's love will compel us to reach out to the needy, help the broken, to seek the lost, and share with the brokenhearted. We will converse with the unkind, walk with the undesirable, make disciples, and love the unlovable.

Luv is a verb.

Go!

- Ashley

REFERENCED VERSES

- Matthew 22:36-40
- John 3:16; 15:13
- Romans 5:8

- 1 Corinthians 13
- 2 Corinthians 5:14-15
- Ephesians 2:4-5
- 1 John 3:1,18; 4:7-11

FOR FURTHER STUDY

- *Crazy Love: Overwhelmed by a Relentless God*, Francis Chan
- *Love is Always Right: A Defense of the One Moral Absolute*, Josh McDowell and Norman Geisler
- *Radical: Taking Back Your Faith from the American Dream*, David Platt
- *The Irresistible Revolution: Living as an Ordinary Radical*, Shane Claiborne
- *The Soul of Hip Hop: Rims, Tims, and a Cultural Theology*, Daniel White Hodge

"JESUS FREAK"

(1995)

Songwriters: Toby McKeehan and Mark Heimermann

Artist: dc Talk

Album: *Jesus Freak*

Proverbs 9:10–The fear of the LORD is the beginning of wisdom, and the knowledge of the Holy One is insight.

Romans 1:16–For I am not ashamed of the gospel, for it is the power of God for salvation to everyone who believes, to the Jew first and also to the Greek.

2 Corinthians 5:9-11–So whether we are at home or away, we make it our aim to please him. For we must all appear before the judgment seat of Christ, so that each one may receive what is due for what he has done in the body, whether good or evil. Therefore, knowing the fear of the Lord, we persuade others.

1 Peter 3:13-17–Now who is there to harm you if you are zealous for what is good? But even if you should suffer for righteousness' sake, you will be blessed. Have no fear of them, nor be troubled, but in your hearts honor Christ the Lord as holy, always being prepared to make a defense to anyone who asks you for a reason for the hope that is in you; yet do it with gentleness and respect, having a good conscience, so that, when you are slandered, those who revile your good behavior in Christ may be put to shame. For it is better to suffer for doing good, if that should be God's will, than for doing evil.

1 Peter 4:4–With respect to this they are surprised when you do not join them in the same flood of debauchery, and they malign you.

1 Peter 4:16–Yet if anyone suffers as a Christian, let him not be ashamed, but let him glorify God in that name.

1 John 3:13–Do not be surprised, brothers, that the world hates you.

90S IMPRESSION

Jesus Freaks are incredibly brave in the face of persecution.

TODAY'S IMPRESSION

Jesus Freaks demonstrate a fear of the Lord that surpasses their fear of man.

How does one write a devotional passage on perhaps the most beloved, most revered song of 90s CCM? For real, what will people think? What if I stumble?

As mentioned in the retrospective true story in this book, "dc Talk Goes Grunge," I still remember the first time that I heard "Jesus

Freak." Its message stirred my young soul like nothing I'd ever heard before. Likewise, many of you may be thinking of your own personal experience with this song. What do you remember?

Even though "Jesus Freak" ignited the hearts of an entire generation of 90s church kids, the term originated decades prior. In the 60s and 70s, "Jesus Freak" was coined to represent another generation of young Christians turning to Jesus during the "One Way" Jesus Revolution. Many young people came to the Lord during this time.

My mother was one of those. At age 16, my mother's friend shared with her a Campus Crusade for Christ tract called "The Four Spiritual Laws." In the quiet halls of her local library, my mother accepted Christ as her Lord. She proudly joined the ranks of the counterculture "Jesus Freaks," and 25 years later, I followed suit.

The term is more than just a song title. It's a call to love Jesus so well that everyone knows you belong to Him. I aspire to be a Jesus Freak. I would consider that as the highest of compliments.

For us Jesus Freaks in America, it's easy to forget that bearing the name of Jesus in other parts of the world can be dangerous and costly. In 1999, dc Talk partnered with the Voice of the Martyrs to do a rebranded version of *Foxe's Book of Martyrs* entitled *Jesus Freaks: Martyrs*. A revised and updated version was published in 2020. As you read through the testimonies of faithful men and women, it's surreal. They don't deny, bow down, or shut up.

They knew what people would say, and they knew what people would do. They followed anyway. Would we do the same?

These ardent enthusiasts of Christ embody the words of David in Psalm 27:

> The LORD is my light and my salvation; whom shall I fear? The LORD is the stronghold of my life; of whom shall I be afraid? (verse 1)

It would seem, then, that these men and women of faith are fearless. Is an absence of fear the secret to their otherworldly bravery? It's very likely these heroes did experience fear. Who wouldn't? Jesus' intense prayers in the garden of Gethsemane in Mark 14 seem to suggest that even Jesus experienced fear and acute anxiety in the moments before His arrest. It's not a sin to feel fear.

Although their fear was probably very real and at times overwhelming, they defeated it with the Holy Spirit and a different kind of fear–the fear of the Lord. Their fear of the Lord was stronger than their fear of man, and this same boldness is possible for the rest of us ordinary people, too.

In Proverbs 9, we learn that "the fear of the LORD is the beginning of wisdom, and the knowledge of the Holy One is insight" (verse 10). In the Old Testament, this fear of the Lord is synonymous with wisdom and obedience to His commands. It's a wisdom firmly anchored in the knowledge that there is only one God, Yahweh. He is righteous and has the authority to judge. This wisdom produces a sense of awe and reverence that yields submission.

This wisdom recognizes that we will account for everything we have ever done. Paul taught in 2 Corinthians 5:9-11:

> So whether we are at home or away, we make it our aim to please him. For we must all appear before the judgment seat of Christ, so that each one may receive what is due for what he has done in the body, whether good or evil. Therefore, knowing the fear of the Lord, we persuade others.

In some translations of verse 11, "fear of the Lord" is translated as "terror of the Lord." Yikes!

While fear is generally an unpleasant experience in life, the fear of the Lord is a gift! From a repentant heart, the fear of the Lord leads to saving faith as we recognize our need for a Savior. We cannot know who we are apart from God or appreciate Christ's rescue of us if it were not for the fear of the Lord.

Do we need the fear of the Lord once saved? Doesn't 1 John 4:18 say, "Perfect love casts out fear?" Yes, and yes. Why, then, would we still need or want the fear of the Lord?

Because of Jesus' loving sacrifice for us, we no longer fear being condemned. Hallelujah! But, let's not forget that there was a time when we were condemned. We cannot let escape from our memory what caused our condemnation in the first place, our sin. The fear of the Lord helps us to remember. We look at the cross and see that our sin has deadly consequences, and His sacrifice becomes all the more meaningful to us. To know the fear of the Lord is to know the perfect love of Christ.

Paul affirmed that it is this sacrificial love of Christ that compels us to love and live as an ambassador for Christ so that others may come to know and be saved as well. His Spirit reminds us of what Jesus has done and empowers us to respond in a way that honors Him (See 2 Corinthians 5:14, 20.).

In Luke 7, Jesus was dining in the home of a Pharisee. A sinful woman from the city saw Jesus sitting at his table. Out in the open, she stood behind Him at His feet and began weeping. Her many tears washed Jesus' dirty and dusty feet. Her hair dried them as she kissed them and anointed them with her valuable oil. Looking upon her in disgust, the Pharisee host mocked her as a sinner unworthy to even touch his guest, Jesus. Jesus turned around to look this woman in the face. With his attention on her, he responded,

> "Do you see this woman? I entered your house; you gave me no water for my feet, but she has wet my feet with her tears and wiped them with her hair. You gave me no kiss, but from the time I came in she has not ceased to kiss my feet. You did not anoint my head with oil, but she has anointed my feet with oint- ment. Therefore I tell you, her sins, which are many, are forgiven—for she loved much. But he who is forgiven little, loves little." And he said to her, "Your sins are forgiven." Then those who were at the table with him began to say among them- selves, "Who is this, who even forgives sins?" And he said to

the woman, "Your faith has saved you; go in peace" (verses 44-50).

Like this precious woman, a Jesus Freak remembers their hopelessness apart from God, which makes the living hope we have in Jesus all the more sweet (See 1 Peter 1:3.). Her tears said it all. Knowing what Jesus did for us changes everything about the way we live and what we know to be important and true. People will certainly label us as strange and weak for admitting we are sinners, but then we get to tell them about the love of our manger-born best friend who saves us.

Still, it's a frightful thing to know what lies ahead for those who do not believe. Are we zealous about our God and what He has done for us? Are we embodying the fear of the Lord in how we live so that others may see and be saved? At the beginning of *Jesus Freaks: Martyrs*, Michael Tait wrote:

> Our mission may not involve hanging on a cross, being jailed, or being burned at the stake here in America, but we have other, more invisible obstacles. Ours is a society built by pride, materialism, and dedication to the status quo. In a world built on free will instead of God's will, we must be the Freaks. While we may not be called to martyr our lives, we must martyr our way of life. We must put our selfish ways to death and march to a different beat. Then the world will see Jesus. (8)

My fellow freaks, hold on to the fear of the Lord so that you will remember what Jesus did for you. Let go of the fear of man, so that they might see Him in you.

Yes, Jesus saves, and let us understand what He saved us from. With no disguises, the fear of the Lord shows us truth and love so powerful that it can overcome the fear of man. Let the world see Jesus in us. Freak for life.

- Rachel

REFERENCED VERSES

- Psalm 27:1
- Proverbs 9:10
- Mark 14
- Luke 7:44-50
- Romans 1:16
- 2 Corinthians 5:9-11, 14, 20
- 1 Peter 3:13-17; 4:4: 4:16
- 1 John 3:13; 4:8

FOR FURTHER STUDY

- *Bearing God's Name: Why Sinai Still Matters*, Carmen Joy Imes
- *Bread for the Resistance: Forty Devotions for Justice People*, Donna Barber
- (For children) *Courage to Run: A Story Based on the Life of Young Harriet Tubman*, Wendy Lawton
- *Jesus Freaks: Stories of Those Who Stood for Jesus, the Ultimate Jesus Freaks*, dc Talk, Voice of the Martyrs
- *The Fear of God*, John Bunyan
- (*https://www.monergism.com/thethreshold/sdg/bunyan/A_Treatise_on_the_Fear_of_God_-_John_Bunyan.pdf*)

LIZ HUMOR

©Liz King

THEOLOGY OF THE HOLY SPIRIT:

HE IS THE LORD OF THE DANCE!

CCM IN KJV?

The KJV-only debate was hot in the 90s. Can you imagine if your favorite 90s Christian songs were written in the style of the 17th-century King James Version (KJV)? We asked our social media followers to make that a reality. See if you can guess the song.

1.

Do not take unto thee the milk of bovines or scoop the saccharine lumps.

They are powerless to console the soul of thyself.

(Susan and Ryan Chesser)

2.

I adore the genre of spoken words set to music.

In the past and yet to come.

If you desire to be among my company, then you best come to an agreement.

That we wilst groove and dance to a booty-shaking and foot-stepping mixture.

(Okie Smith)

3.

What therefore shall the people conclude when they find that I am a Jesus zealot?

(Jesse Edmondson)

4.

Yea, verily, our God art an awesome God.

He reigneth from yon Heaven above

Full of all wisdom beyond all sages, omnipotence, and charity

Our God art an awesome God most verily.

(Nathan Ludwick)

5.

Thou art beholden to like it;

Thou art beholden to love it.

Thou knowest thou needest a modicum of Jesus in thy life.

(Sarah Awa)

6.

Lavishly our lives art wasted

Humbleness hath been untast'd

Thee cannot liveth thy life to prithee thyself, aye

Yond is a tip from mine own mistakes

Precisely what it doth taketh not

To win thee has't did get to cometh in lasteth position

To liveth thy life thee has't get to loseth

And all the los'rs receiveth a coronet

Down I went and that Gent lifts me up

Down I went and that Gent lifts me up

Down I went and that Gent lifts me up

I doth went down

(Jon Waley)

7.

How come I didn't go the distance and try to impress thee

But rather was satisfying thine self?

When all is said and done, and thou heart is shattered

I view the error of attempting to impress thine own ways.

(Paul Portell)

8.

Though the night grow long and the darkness grow deep, extinguish
not thy candle.

(David Ryerson)

9.

Who thou be in thy dwelling?

Who thou be in thy dwelling?

Tis' J period C period.

(Brian Walters)

10.

I beseech thee, brethren,

Saddle ye horses!

Blazeth the trail before thee.

Answer Key:

1. "Breakfast in Hell," Newsbards
2. "I Luv Rap Music," Duke and Count Talk
3. "Jesus Freak," Duke and Count Talk
4. "Awesome God," Lord Richard of Mullins
5. "Like It, Love It, Need It," Duke and Count Talk
6. "Get Down," Audio Achdukes
7. "Great Lengths," PF of R
8. "Keep the Candle Burning," Ladies of Point Grace
9. "Who's in the House," Earl of Carman
10. "The Great Adventure," Sir Steven Curtis Chapfellow

"CONSUMING FIRE"

(1995)

Songwriter: Mac Powell

Artist: Third Day

Album: *Third Day*

> **Hebrews 12:28-29**–Therefore let us be grateful for receiving a kingdom that cannot be shaken, and thus let us offer to God acceptable worship, with reverence and awe, for our God is a consuming fire.

90S IMPRESSION

The Holy Spirit is like a consuming fire.

TODAY'S IMPRESSION

The Holy Spirit's consuming fire will burn away that which doesn't belong in His kingdom.

⊱⊰

The year 1995 was such a great year for 90s CCM rock. This is the year we were blessed with *Jesus Freak*, Petra's *No Doubt*, Jars of Clay's debut, and, a lesser-known independent-label debut album from a Georgia band called Third Day. Quickly snatched up by a bigger record label, Third Day's debut album was re-released in 1996 with the memorable bus album cover that we all know and love.

These guys were not a *Jesus Freak* ripple effect. With a southern flare, their sound was original and bold. This was something fresh, something different. This isn't Sandi Patty. This isn't Wayne Watson. As much as we love those CCM pioneers, the youth of the day were ready for something new. Hopping on the Third Day bus, we were ready for the ride.

On their debut album, Third Day kicks it off with their single "Consuming Fire." As both a prayer and an exhortation, the lyrics invite us to think about how God is a consuming fire that reaches the deepest parts of our souls. Where does this imagery come from?

In Deuteronomy, Moses reminded the Israelites of their special covenant with Yahweh. Of all the peoples of the earth, this set of people was chosen to bear His name (See Deuteronomy 7:6.). These were holy people set apart for the Lord.

As part of their covenant, God gave them His law at Mount Sinai. The mountain appeared to burn with His presence.

> Now the appearance of the glory of the LORD was like a devouring fire on the top of the mountain in the sight of the people of Israel (Exodus 24:17).

The Israelites were scared to death of what they saw. It must have been a frightful sight.

"And you said, 'Behold, the LORD our God has shown us his glory and greatness, and we have heard his voice out of the midst of the fire. This day we have seen God speak with man, and man still live. Now therefore why should we die? For this great fire will consume us. If we hear the voice of the LORD our God any more, we shall die. For who is there of all flesh, that has heard the voice of the living God speaking out of the midst of fire as we have, and has still lived?" (Deuteronomy 5:24-26).

When Moses was in his final days, he urged the Israelites to remember the greatest commandment of the law, "You shall love the LORD your God with all your heart and with all your soul and with all your might" (Deuteronomy 6:5). They were warned against idolatry and reminded that "the LORD your God is a consuming fire, a jealous God" (4:24). They know this is true because they saw the terrifying consuming fire with their own eyes.

God's response to idolatry is His consuming fire wrath. This is a God who will not stand for competition. There is only one God, Yahweh. He demands and deserves all of your heart, soul, and might.

In 1925, preacher and pastor Arthur W. Pink expounds in *The Attributes of God* that God's wrath is evidence of God's perfect divine nature and encourages us to meditate on it frequently. Pink explained that when we meditate on God's wrath, three things will occur.

First, we will hate sin.

> We are prone to regard sin lightly, to gloss over its hideousness, to make excuses for it. But the more we study and ponder God's abhorrence of sin and His frightful vengeance upon it, the more likely we are to realize its heinousness.

Second, we will gain godly fear.

> We cannot serve Him acceptably unless there is due reverence for His awful Majesty and godly fear of His righteous anger;

these are best promoted by frequently calling to mind that "our God is a consuming fire."

Third, we will be compelled to praise God.

> ...to draw out our souls in fervent praise for our having been delivered from the "wrath to come" (1 Thessalonians 1:10).

The author of Hebrews taught his early Christian readers to think upon God's wrath, His consuming fire. His Jewish Christian audience would immediately think of Mount Sinai when they heard the phrase "consuming fire." Hebrews 12:28-29:

> Therefore let us be grateful for receiving a kingdom that cannot be shaken, and thus let us offer to God acceptable worship, with reverence and awe, for our God is a consuming fire.

God's consuming fire will burn away that which doesn't belong in His kingdom.

For the unbeliever, God's consuming fire of wrath leads to destruction. But for those who have been saved from God's wrath through Jesus, the consuming fire leads to life and righteousness. No longer destroyed by its flames, we are purified by it as our cold hearts of stone are replaced with hearts that can beat for Him (See Ezekiel 11:19; 36:26.). His purifying fire seeks out what needs to be destroyed in our lives, so what is eternal will remain and will yield "fruit of right-eousness" (See Hebrews 12:11.).

God can use trials of suffering, loving discipline, or other forms of training to refine our faith with fire (See 1 Peter 1:6-7.). While it may be painful at the time, His work is not in vain (See Romans 8:28.).

The song asks us twice if we realize that inside each of us is a flame. A consuming fire is powerful. Through the Spirit, you have that same energy living in you and it is through His energy that you will make it through the Refiner's fire (See Colossians 1:29.).

Are you meditating on our Almighty God's holiness and perfection? Are you allowing His flames to burn away that which doesn't belong deep in your soul? Meditating on His wrath trains us to abhor sin, practice awe and reverence, and compels us to praise. Will you let it burn?

- Rachel

REFERENCED VERSES

- Exodus 24:17
- Deuteronomy 5:24-26; 6:5; 7:6
- Ezekiel 11:19; 36:26
- Colossians 1:29
- 1 Thessalonians 1:10
- Hebrews 12:11; 12:28-29
- 1 Peter 1:6-7

FOR FURTHER STUDY

- *The Attributes of God*, A.W. Pink (*https://www.monergism.com/thethreshold/sdg/attributes_online.html*)
- *The Fire of God's Presence: Drawing Near to a Holy God*, A. W. Tozer

"UNDER THE INFLUENCE"

(1996)

Songwriter: Mark Heimermann

Artist: Anointed

Album: *Under the Influence*

2 Corinthians 5:17–Therefore, if anyone is in Christ, he is a new creation. The old has passed away; behold, the new has come.

Galatians 5:22-23–But the fruit of the Spirit is love, joy, peace, patience, kindness, goodness, faithfulness, gentleness, self-control; against such things there is no law.

2 Peter 1:3-4–His divine power has granted to us all things that pertain to life and godliness, through the knowledge of him who called us to his own glory and excellence, by which he has granted to us his precious and very great promises, so that through them you may become partakers of the divine nature, having escaped from the corruption that is in the world because of sinful desire.

90S IMPRESSION

I need the Holy Spirit to make me more like Jesus.

TODAY'S IMPRESSION

The Holy Spirit has transformed my Spirit.

ᐳᐁᐁᐧ ᐸ ᐊᐸᐳᐯ

Who's ready for some epic harmony? In 1996, the trio (now a duo) Anointed released their third album with the title track "Under the Influence." The chorus tells us that they are under the influence of love. It speaks of giving up control and acknowledges that we are not our own. We rest knowing that we are under the covering of His grace and love. It's a great message artistically delivered.

An interesting use of the phrase "under the influence," this song challenges me to consider how God continually works in my life to bring about His purposes for me and His kingdom. To me, that speaks of the work of the Holy Spirit. In Galatians, Paul challenged the believers in Galatia to walk in the Spirit as opposed to living under the law. Are you under His influence? How would you know?

A life walking in the Spirit will have beautiful fruit to show for it. If you grew up in the church, you may have even memorized this passage from Galatians 5:22-23,

> "But the fruit of the Spirit is love, joy, peace, patience, kindness, goodness, faithfulness, gentleness, self-control; against such things there is no law."

As a youngster, you may have been taught to emulate these traits, or fruits, like a checklist. We were admonished to be loving, joyful, peaceful…you get the idea. Act kind and patient to your annoying sibling. Act good when your parents tell you not to sass your grandmother. In other words, perform well and get that spiritual gold star like a good little boy or girl!

Well, good luck with that, homeskillet. Fruit of the Spirit is a work of the Spirit, not of ourselves. It is so much more than just good deeds.

Paul calls it the "fruit of the Spirit." These are not "fruits" of the Spirit but simply the "fruit" of the Spirit. I often see the word "character qualities" or "virtues" used to describe the fruit. To me, these terms fall short of how transformational the fruit is. For example, unbelievers can be very outwardly virtuous, but they do not have the fruit of the Spirit.

What is the difference then?

The fruit is more than a list of character traits. Rather, it's the result of a whole spiritual metamorphosis. If you are born again, fruit isn't just what you do, it is who you are through His Spirit. You don't just show love, you are loving. You don't just show joy, you are joyful. You don't just show peace, you are peaceful.

In Jesus, your inclinations and your tendencies are completely new. His Spirit transforms you from the inside out. From your outward motivations to your innermost thoughts, the Spirit fundamentally changes how you live and breathe. This is His fruit-bearing in you, and it is for His glory. Hallelujah!

If you have the fruit of the Spirit, something miraculous has happened and it goes way beyond just works.

The Spirit isn't interested in just making us moral people. Boy Scouts and Girl Scouts can do that. The law shows us that moral living and good works aren't enough to change our corrupt spiritual disposition. We need the work of a Savior (See Galatians 2:21; 5:18.).

See, we have this flesh. The flesh is our natural state apart from the Holy Spirit. Our flesh and God's Spirit are always contrary to one another (See Galatians 5:17.). What flesh produces is pretty nasty and so contrary to God's law (See Galatians 5:19-21.). Not surprisingly, John 12:24 says that if we desire to bear fruit, our flesh must die.

"Truly, truly, I say to you, unless a grain of wheat falls into the earth and dies, it remains alone; but if it dies, it bears much fruit."

Fruit of the Spirit is the result of us joining Jesus from death to life. Through Jesus, we joyfully acknowledge that our flesh has been crucified (See Galatians 2:20.). And, we are born again with His Spirit-filled life. As that same Spirit bears fruit in us, we become more like our crucified and risen Savior. He makes us new creations, baby (See 2 Corinthians 5:17.).

This is the fundamental difference between a "moral character trait" and the fruit of the Spirit: The fruit of the Spirit is a Christ-like disposition that can love God and love others as He has commanded us.

"If you abide in me, and my words abide in you, ask whatever you wish, and it will be done for you. By this my Father is glorified, that you bear much fruit and so prove to be my disciples. As the Father has loved me, so have I loved you. Abide in my love. If you keep my commandments, you will abide in my love, just as I have kept my Father's commandments and abide in his love. These things I have spoken to you, that my joy may be in you, and that your joy may be full. This is my commandment, that you love one another as I have loved you" (John 15:7-12).

Fulfilling this commandment can only be accomplished by the Spirit in us. Christ in us is where we place our faith and certainly not in the flesh. As if.

But dang that flesh! My flesh isn't loving, joyful, or peaceful. My flesh has a big mouth and a short temper. Martin Luther compared the indwelling sin to a man's beard. Got a smooth shave today? Just wait until tomorrow. Remembering that our flesh is dead is like taking a daily shave. When the sin appears, we've got to resist and cut it off.

As born again Christians, we must remember the new creation that we are. The fruit of the Spirit is in us because Jesus is in us. Keep going back and remembering that our old nature has been crucified. Our regeneration has made us free and fruity.

Does your life exhibit works of the flesh or fruit of the Spirit? Honestly, there could be outward signs of both. Take heart, God is still working on all of us. Even though our spirit has been made new, old habits die hard. We must pray that His Spirit would lead us away from the desires of the flesh and toward our Savior. His Word will be the light to our path (See Psalm 119:105.). Surely He will do it (See 1 Thessalonians 5:23.).

How exciting it is to see when the Spirit bears this marvelous fruit. Even more so, how joyous it is to experience it. Throw away the check-list and pick up your walking stick. Walk in the Spirit. Bearing His fruit, you are under His influence of love.

- Rachel

REFERENCED VERSES

- Psalm 119:105
- John 12:24; 15:7-12
- 2 Corinthians 5:17
- Galatians 2:21; 5:17-23
- 2 Thessalonians 5:23
- 2 Peter 1:3-4

FOR FURTHER STUDY

- *Hymns of the Spirit: The Trinity Project Book 3*, Cameron Frank, Preston Norman, and Nathan Drake
- *The Doctrine of Repentance*, Thomas Watson (*https://www.moner-gism.com/doctrine-repentance-ebook*)

"OPEN THE EYES OF MY HEART"

(1999)

Songwriter: Paul Boloche

Artist: Sonicflood

Album: *Sonicflood*

Ephesians 1:16-23–I do not cease to give thanks for you, remembering you in my prayers, that the God of our Lord Jesus Christ, the Father of glory, may give you the Spirit of wisdom and of revelation in the knowledge of him, having the eyes of your hearts enlightened, that you may know what is the hope to which he has called you, what are the riches of his glorious inheritance in the saints, and what is the immeasurable greatness of his power toward us who believe, according to the working of his great might that he worked in Christ when he raised him from the dead and seated him at his right hand in the heavenly places, far above all rule and authority and power and dominion, and above every name that is named, not only in this age but also in the one to come. And he put all things under his feet and gave him as head over all things to the church, which is his body, the fullness of him who fills all in all.

90S IMPRESSION

God opens the eyes of hearts so that we can worship Him and trust Him in our lives.

TODAY'S IMPRESSION

God awakens us to the reality of our sin and the hope of the gospel. When Jesus opens our eyes in a spiritual sense, we can trust in Him as Savior and live a life of worship. We get to live life "seeing Jesus!"

Sonicflood's 1999 self-titled album was a game-changer and one of the most influential albums in Christian music over the last several decades. Those are strong words, but that is the way I see it! The album opened a flood of sonic worship in churches and youth groups everywhere.

Many songs off the album became staples for midweek youth worship services, and many of those same songs began to spill over into what I called, as a kid, "big church." Imagine one album influencing us all to start singing "I Can Sing of Your Love Forever," "Heart of Worship," "I Want to Know You," and "Holiness." But more than the influence of the songs we sang was the movement that took place with CCM bands and artists.

Everyone started producing worship albums, and the rest is history. I can talk about whether that was good or bad for CCM and argue from both sides, which is neither here nor there. No matter our thoughts on the matter, it happened. It also ushered in bands known for producing strictly worship music, and their albums got consistent airplay on Christian radio. Turn on your local Christian radio station today, and you will hear a constant "flood" of many talented worship bands.

Such was Sonicflood. "Open the Eyes of My Heart" rivaled only "Heart of Worship" in popularity, in my estimation. (OK, one can make a case for "I Could Sing of Your Love Forever.") The band brought popularity to a song written by worship leader and recording artist Paul Baloche, and the song made its way to one of his praise albums soon thereafter. And, then, of course, it has been covered countless times.

So, let's get to the spiritual insight. Granted, it seems to be a simple song. One could criticize the praise chorus and claim it to be typical of modern praise music, fairly repetitive. That is sometimes fair although, in many well-loved hymns, the chorus is repeated as well. (Enter "Love Lifted Me"–one of my favorites, actually!)

Sure, we sing "Open the Eyes of My Heart" repeatedly. If we peel back the repetition of the chorus, a biblical passage is being repeated that warrants our attention. The chorus is unapologetically scriptural and theologically profound.

In Ephesians 1:17-18, Paul stated, "The Father of glory, may give you the Spirit of wisdom and of revelation in the knowledge of him, having the eyes of your hearts enlightened, that you may know what is the hope to which he has called you." Paul prayed that God would open the eyes of their hearts. It is almost word for word what Paul Baloche reiterated.

The song asks God to open the eyes of our hearts so that we would see Him. "Hearts with eyes" is incredible imagery because, if you have looked in an anatomy and physiology book lately, hearts don't have eyes.

Yet, they do.

Our hearts see things in ways that our physical eyes can't. Our hearts can see, or not see, God. Our hearts can see pain, and our hearts can see love. The figurative eyes of our hearts are the window into who we are spiritually and enable us to be awakened to the reality of Christ when the vision of Jesus is before them.

Thus, Paul asked that these cardiovascular eyes see Jesus. To be sure, that is precisely what must happen for someone to come to faith in Christ.

God opens the eyes of our hearts to see Him. In John 9, Jesus healed a man who had been blind from birth. Though a story of actual healing, I see the story as a living parable, or metaphor, for the gospel.

We are all born blind. We can't see God and are unable in our abilities to do so unless God opens our eyes to see Him. The theological doctrine known as Original Sin, closely tied to Total Depravity, teaches this idea, and Scripture testifies to these truths in numerous places.

In Psalm 51:5, after the Bathsheba incident, King David confessed that he was "brought forth in iniquity." In sin, his mother conceived him. He didn't become a sinner as he lived life and made sinful choices. He was born a sinner. In Romans 5, Paul explained how we all inherited sin from Adam. Adam was the original sinner, and we all inherit sin passed down from his seed. Every human who ever lived, except Jesus, inherited Adam's sin nature which originated from the fall. It takes another Adam, who represents us a second time, for us to overcome this sin and find forgiveness. This last Adam, Jesus, fixes what the first Adam messed up. We are born totally depraved because of the sin of the first Adam. God forgives us when we profess faith in the life, death, and resurrection of the last Adam, Jesus Christ.

However, we are blind to this truth and cannot see it or understand it until God opens the eyes of our hearts to see it. Quoting the Old Testament in Romans 3:10-12, Paul emphasized that no one is righteous. Not one! Due to our unrighteousness, we cannot see God and deserve death. Oh, the overwhelming grace of God that opens our eyes to our sin and the person of Jesus Christ. He opens the eyes of our hearts so that we can see Him!

As the healing goes in John 9, so does our spiritual healing. God restores our sight spiritually through His Son! And, just as the man who receives sight, we proclaim Jesus when we see His amazing grace. The words of that faithful hymn never grow old and speak the greatest truth and testimonial ever: "Amazing Grace, how sweet the sound, that saved a wretch like me! I once was lost, but now am found; was blind, but now I see."

Also, the beauty of grace is that this isn't just about salvation. Once we see Jesus, we pray that God continually opens the eyes of our hearts so we can see Him high and lifted up. When we see Him and acknowledge His majesty, we also desire to lift Him up. We illuminate in His glorious light!

One of the beautiful aspects of being rescued from the sin inherited from Adam by the work of Jesus as our Savior is that, in turn, we will live lives of worship! Our desire to lift up Jesus is greatly motivated by our thankfulness in the rescue that took place.

This kind of worship goes far beyond Wednesday night youth group or "big church." When we walk with Jesus and truly see Him, we will seek to worship Him in all of life as we live for Him. True life is living in Christ (See Philippians 1:21.)! His life is now our life (See Colossians 3:4.)! Spiritual fruit will grow from us as we abide in the living Christ. The life lived trusting in Jesus will reflect that He is our very life! As I look to Jesus or "see" Him, as the lyrics state, I want to worship and live for Him (See Romans 12:1-2.).

As Jesus opens the eyes of our hearts, our prayer is that He would pour out His power and love to us, our churches, and the world around us. As He does so, we join with the angels in Heaven in worship, proclaiming, "Holy, Holy, Holy!"

- Ashley

REFERENCED VERSES

- Psalm 51:5
- John 9–10
- Romans 3:10-12; 5:12-21; 12:1-2
- Ephesians 1:16-23
- Philippians 1:21
- Colossians 3:4

FOR FURTHER STUDY

- *Captured by Grace: No One is Beyond the Reach of a Loving God*, David Jeremiah
- *Faith Alone: The Doctrine of Justification*, Thomas R. Schreiner
- *God's Greater Glory: The Exalted God of Scripture and the Christian Faith*, Bruce Ware
- *Hymns of the Father: The Trinity Project Book 1*, Cameron Frank, Preston Norman, and Nathan Drake
- *Proof: Finding Freedom Through the Intoxicating Joy of Irresistible Grace*, Daniel Montgomery and Timothy Paul Jones
- *The Dialogue of Worship: Creating Space for Revelation and Response*, Gary A. Furr and Milburn Price
- *Worship in Spirit and Truth: A Refreshing Study of the Principles and Practices of Biblical Worship*, John M. Frame

LIZ HUMOR

Newsboys "Entertaining Angels"

©Liz King

THEOLOGY OF THE NEW HEAVEN & THE NEW EARTH:

IT'S GOLDIE'S LAST DAY.

LIZ HUMOR

Growing up in the 90s, kids were triggered by three simple words. The fear was real. No one wanted to hear those words for any reason!
Mom!! Have you seen my Gameboy? Last time I saw it, it was at Grandmas.
F.F.H.
No honey. Maybe it...
GOT LEFT BEHIND!!!
NOOOOO!!!
©Liz King

COMICALLY INSPIRED

90S CHRISTIAN CULTURE THROUGH A COMEDIC LENS

Hey friends, I'm Liz King. I'm the creator of Liz Humor Comics, the cartoons you've seen throughout the pages of this book. I'm a stay-at-home mom in Bowling Green, Kentucky.

Having grown up in a strict religious home, I didn't know about Contemporary Christian music until my later teen years. Someone from high school slipped me a dc Talk tape, and it changed everything for me. I've loved this music ever since.

Artists such as dc Talk, Rebecca St. James, Newsboys, T-Bone, Bride, Michael W. Smith, Steven Curtis Chapman, and Skillet have a special place in my heart. Their works have influenced my faith more than words can say. That's why I drew it instead!

I took inspiration for the comics from my own experiences in 90s Christian culture along with my love for God and the golden age of Christian music. You'll probably discover that God blessed me with a twisted sense of humor. I had a blast creating each one! I hope you have enjoyed them.

Come find me on Instagram, Facebook, and TikTok @LizHumorComics.

"You Know Who's Doin It?"

- Liz King

LIZ HUMOR

© Liz King

"ANOTHER TIME, ANOTHER PLACE"

(1990)

Songwriter: Gary Driskell

Artist: Sandi Patty and Wayne Watson

Album: *Another Time, Another Place*

Revelation 21:1-4–Then I saw a new heaven and a new earth, for the first heaven and the first earth had passed away, and the sea was no more. And I saw the holy city, new Jerusalem, coming down out of heaven from God, prepared as a bride adorned for her husband. And I heard a loud voice from the throne saying, "Behold, the dwelling place of God is with man. He will dwell with them, and they will be his people, and God himself will be with them as their God. He will wipe away every tear from their eyes, and death shall be no more, neither shall there be mourning, nor crying, nor pain anymore, for the former things have passed away."

90S IMPRESSION

Someday when this life is over, I get to go to Heaven.

TODAY'S IMPRESSION

God has something planned for those who He redeemed that is beyond what we could ever imagine. Until that time, we wait with expectation and trust in Him. What He has revealed to us in His Word about the New Heaven and New Earth are promises in which we can find great peace as we partake in His goodness in this life.

I can picture it like it was yesterday. The first notes of Sandi Patty and Wayne Watson's "Another Time, Another Place" rang out as a breathtaking image of an oceanic sunrise appeared. I was a senior in high school, and my student pastor prepared a senior slideshow on a Wednesday night in celebration of the graduates, of which I was one. That first slide was from a retreat to Panama City Beach, Florida, and as the rest of the pictures scrolled, the tears flowed. I don't even remember if my youth pastor used Smitty's "Friends" in the show, but it didn't matter!

"Another Time, Another Place" has always held a nostalgic place in my heart. I reminisce on the blessings of student ministry, mission trips, retreats, and my friends. To be honest, this song is probably in my top two or three favorite Christian songs of all time.

Looking back, feeling those feelings, and thinking about those memories is something I enjoy doing. However, this song is not about looking back. It is about anticipation and what lies ahead!

Many years have passed since that day in 1992, and I have experienced a great deal more of what life has to offer. So much of it is so good, and I feel blessed beyond measure. There are days when I would say I'm living the dream! But, in a world plagued by sin, I have also seen the bad and experienced the bad. As a pastor, I've walked with many people through horrific things that leave me broken and longing for something beyond what this life offers.

As we look forward, we remind ourselves that we already know the blessing of Jesus, now! When we receive eternal life, the eternal life of Jesus comes to live in us immediately. Whoever believes in Him not only receives the blessing of eternity but also gets the eternal Jesus coming to reside in us! As we discussed in "Beauty for Ashes," God gives us all we need.

But even in that, we long for Heaven. We wait for Heaven. Another time and another place exists for the Christian, and sometimes waiting is the hardest part.

Paul's words in the first chapter of his letter to the church in Colossae, "Christ in you, the hope of glory," bring both thoughts together (Colossians 1:27). We get the glory of knowing Jesus now, ensuring that something glorious awaits beyond this life. The hope of glory reminds us that total restoration awaits, so we put our hope in Him.

So, there is the here, and the hereafter.

A question people often ask is, *What is Heaven like?* There is a lot we know and a lot we don't know. We must always look to God's Word when searching for the answers to questions of eternity. And, just so you know, I'm always very skeptical and reluctant to use any resources or testimonies of those who "died and came back." There may be some great truths in their experiences, but there is often stuff that the Bible just doesn't say when compared to their testimonials. We should be cautious about gleaning our theology of Heaven from sources other than God's Word.

In Revelation, Jesus talks about the new time and place in which Sandi and Wayne sing. What is this place? What is it like? What are we waiting for?

I can't even scratch the surface of the biblical possibilities in a short devotion. We know we will get new, glorified bodies (See Philippians

3:21.)! That sounds good because it has been some (ahem) years since 1992, and my aging, unglorified body is hurting!

We know that "the whole creation has been groaning together in the pains of childbirth until now," and that there will be a New Heaven and New Earth (See Romans 8:22-29.). So it is not just about new bodies! The New Heaven and New Earth will not display the repercussions of sin, and Jesus will light the entire place up! I believe from the Bible that we can ascertain that we will eat and drink, enjoy relationships like never before, learn, explore, and enjoy the beauty of God in unimaginable ways. It will be personal, and it will be worshipful. We will have fruitful lives, and the blessings of eternity will be more than we can dream up. What God has planned for us is beyond measure.

The hereafter is sounding like "the bomb!"

When we look at the core truth of Revelation 21, the greatest assurance in the hereafter is the fact that God is making all things new. He makes us new now, and in the end, He is making all things new.

But, we do enjoy things now, right? The Bible is clear that every good and perfect gift comes from God. How much more will we enjoy the things God has made new in eternity? The beauty of creation, the love of relationships, the exquisiteness of art, the joy of accomplishment and camaraderie, the blessing of fulfilling work, and the excitement of growing in knowledge are amazing gifts. And, although this is about "Another Time, Another Place," we might even have a "big, big" yard to play football!

In the sovereignty of God, the sky's the limit in His new creation. Most of all, God will bless us with His presence, and the enjoyment of His blessings will overflow in eternity like the river flowing through the heavenly city!

And, what does my heart yearn for the most when I envision Heaven? Jesus' promise in Revelation 21: "God himself will be with them as their God. He will wipe away every tear from their eyes, and death shall be no more, neither shall there be mourning, nor crying, nor pain anymore, for the former things have passed away"(verses 3-4).

Can you imagine? No more crying or pain, and all the bad stuff passed away. Now that is something that my heart burns for!

God not only removes the tears and pain. Our Lord makes all things new, not just better, in the New Heaven and New Earth. New! The slightest speck of sin will not exist in Heaven, meaning suffering and hardship are non-existent. Death is no more! God finally renews everything in all of creation, and the New Heaven and the New Earth are the place of perfection where the Lamb of God forever dwells with His Bride!

We will reside in eternity in the completion of God's eternal plan to be with His people. All things will be new, and Jesus will fulfill His big, big story. As the song states, the ultimate joy of Heaven will be when we look in the face of Jesus! (That's the next devotion!)

Revelation 22 speaks of seeing Jesus' face as we dwell with Him in His forever reign. These last two chapters of Revelation involve the majesty of God and the beauty of being God's redeemed people. Jesus has made all things new, and we will reside in a new, perfect place as we see Jesus as never before! To quote another CCM classic by MercyMe, "I Can Only Imagine!"

Right now, we get to taste and see the goodness of God, and it is real and tangible. In eternity, the feast of all feasts will take place as we dine with the Savior. The presence of sin will be no more, and the reality of our Lord who prepared the place where we dwell will make our hearts explode in eternal bliss!

I am waiting for that day! Jesus made it clear in John 14 that we get there through the blood of Jesus. May we walk with the Way, Truth, and Life now, knowing we will run on the streets of gold in His presence forever!

- Ashley

REFERENCED VERSES

- John 14
- Romans 8:22-29
- Philippians 3:21
- Colossians 1:27
- Revelation 21–22

FOR FURTHER STUDY

- *Heaven: A Comprehensive Guide to Everything the Bible Says About Our Eternal Home*, Randy Alcorn
- *Unseen Realities: Heaven, Hell, Angels and Demons*, R.C. Sproul

"I WILL BE FREE"

(1993)

Songwriter: Cindy Morgan

Artist: Cindy Morgan

Album: *A Reason to Live*

1 John 3:2–Beloved, we are God"s children now, and what we will be has not yet appeared; but we know that when he appears we shall be like him, because we shall see him as he is.

90S IMPRESSION

One day, I will be free in Heaven.

TODAY'S IMPRESSION

At my glorification, I will be completely free because I will be like Jesus.

Cindy Morgan's gorgeous song "I Will Be Free" is what we've chosen to end this theological mixtape we've enjoyed together. In Cindy's sweeping chorus, we run the mountains, drink from the living fountain, and we keep moving forward because our Savior is waiting for us. We will reach Him, and when we see Him, we will be free. The work He is doing in us, which we have explored throughout the pages of this book, will be complete (See Philippians 1:6.).

As we have mixtape theologized together, we have explored key doctrines. Because of the cross, Heaven is in the real world. Because of His resurrection, Jesus makes a new way to be human. We are crucified with Christ, and there is now no condemnation. On this great adventure, we surrender all. He'll lead us home.

If your faith in Jesus was a song, how would it sound? What would it say?

Jesus is the beginning and end note for our faith song. He is the composer, the melody, and the lyric repeated in every verse and chorus.. As believers, we are gifted this song of love to sing and to make our own. We sing it to Him, each other, and the world. As we sing it, we give glory to the Son and have great hope that, one day, we will be with and like the One who composed it.

The believers' song is a royal anthem about a King who adopted us (Romans 8:15). Galatians 4:7 declares, "So you are no longer a slave, but a son, and if a son, then an heir through God." We were once slaves, but are free. Not only free, but we are also heirs to the kingdom.

Our hymn concludes with our glorification–the theological term for this final event when we become like our Savior. At that moment, the King's work of our sanctification will be finished. First John 3:2 promises,

> Beloved, we are God's children now, and what we will be has not yet appeared; but we know that when he appears we shall be like him, because we shall see him as he is.

The battle between flesh and spirit will be over. We will experience the freedom we long for.

Our glorification occurs the moment we see Jesus. Just reading those words, "seeing Jesus," brings so much hope and anticipation. In 1856 Charles Spurgeon preached his sermon "The Beatific Vision,"

> The thing for which I would pray above all others, would be forever to behold His face, forever to lay my head upon His breast, forever to know that I am His, forever to dwell with Him. Ay, one short glimpse, one transitory vision of His glory, one brief glance at his marred, but now exalted and beaming countenance, would repay almost a world of trouble.

Some theologians refer to glorification as the final chain in the Golden Chain of Redemption from Romans 8:29-30. We were predestined, called, justified, and eventually glorified. Can you imagine a greater conclusion to your faith song than to see Jesus and to share in His likeness forever?

Spurgeon pondered what it might be like when we see our Lord and Savior face to face. Rejoice in these wonderful truths. Can you imagine what he described?

> You may trust the believer for knowing His Master when he finds Him. We shall not need to have Jesus Christ introduced to us when we go to heaven, for if He were off His throne and sitting down with all the rest of the blessed spirits, we should go up to Him directly and say, "Jesus I know You." The devil knew Him, for he said, "Jesus I know," and I am sure God's people ought to know Him.
>
> "Jesus I know You," we shall say at once, as we go up to Him. "How do you know Me?" says Jesus. "Why, sweet Jesus, we are no strangers. You have manifested Yourself to me as You do not unto the world. You have given me sometimes such tokens of your gracious affection, do you think I have forgotten You? Why, I have seen Your hands and Your feet sometimes by faith,

and I have put my hand into Your side, like Thomas of old, and think You that I am a stranger to You? No, blessed Jesus, if You were to put Your hand before Your eyes, and hide Your countenance I should know You then. Were You blindfolded once more, my eyes would tell you, for I have known You too long to doubt Your personality."

Believer, take this thought with you, "We shall see Him," despite all the changes in His position. It will be the same person. We shall see the same hands that were pierced, the same feet that were weary, the same lips that preached, the same eyes that wept, the same heart that heaved with agony–positively the same, except as to His condition. "We shall see Him." Write the word Him as large as you like. "We shall see Him as He is."

Finally, at this event of our complete regeneration, we will truly reflect Him as He originally intended for His imagers to do, to be perfect as He is perfect.

We can sing our faith song with confidence and with conviction. We will miss some notes here and there, but one day, we will look upon our Lord and finally be able to play it perfectly and freely to Him. I can't wait to hear that mixtape.

- Rachel

REFERENCED VERSES

- Romans 8:15
- Galatians 4:7
- Philippians 1:6
- 1 John 3:2

FOR FURTHER STUDY

- *Blessed: Experiencing the Promise of the Book of Revelation,* Nancy Guthrie
- *Glorification: An Introduction,* Graham A. Cole and Oren R. Martin
- "The Beatific Vision," Charles Spurgeon (*https://www.spurgeon.org/resource-library/sermons/the-beatific-vision*)

PASS OR FAIL:

THE DEFINITIVE 90S CCM POP QUIZ

In the words of Knowdaverbs, "Yo, it's time for class." How much 90s Christian music trivia do you know? We combed through Mark Allen Powell's *Encyclopedia of Contemporary Christian Music* to create one doozy of a quiz. We hope you have studied. Pick up your #2 pencil, kids. Your exam begins now.

1. Which dude is not one of the Gotee Brothers?

    1. Toby McKeehan
    2. Joey Elwood
    3. Mark Stuart
    4. Todd Collins

2. Which Chapman(s) won a Dove Award for Country Album?

    1. Steven Curtis Chapman
    2. Steve and Annie Chapman

3. Gary Chapman
4. All of the above

3. Which artist wrote the music for Rebecca St. James' first hit, "Here I Am"?

1. Eric Champion
2. Sandi Patty
3. Wayne Kirkpatrick
4. Twila Paris

4. Which band includes a professional surfer, who has been on the cover of *Surfing* magazine numerous times?

1. Switchfoot
2. O.C. Supertones
3. The Insyderz
4. Dakoda Motor Co.

5. Which artist/band has a secret song about exploring the potential for alien life on Pluto?

1. Plumb
2. Johnny Q. Public
3. The Elms
4. Hokus Pick Manouver

6. Five Iron Frenzy took part in a tour called "Ska against _____"

   1. Hunger
   2. Racism
   3. AIDS
   4. Sellouts

7. Which band's frontman has founded a Christian ministry called Groundworks Ministries to equip Christians to read one chapter of the Bible every day?

   1. Big Tent Revival's Steve Wiggins
   2. All Star United's Ian Eskelin
   3. Mukala's Dan Mukala
   4. NewSong's Russ Lee

8. Which band had a band member's mother as their manager?

   1. P.O.D.
   2. Starflyer 59
   3. Whitecross
   4. MxPx

9. Which all-female group had an endorsement deal with cosmetics company Revlon?

   1. Trin-i-tee 5:7
   2. Out of Eden
   3. Mary Mary
   4. Zoe Girl

. . .

10. Which college was the location where both Bleach and Audio Adrenaline were formed?

1. Toccoa Falls College
2. Kentucky Christian College
3. Anderson University
4. University of Alabama

11. Which artist was described as "evangelical rock's court jester" by *Newsweek*?

1. Steve Taylor
2. Mark Lowry
3. Russ Taff
4. Larry Norman

12. Which group has been featured on albums by Stevie Wonder, Don Henley, and Kenny Rogers while also recording the theme song for the television series *Murphy Brown*?

1. Take 6
2. The Winans
3. God's Property
4. Commissioned

13. How did Petra members John Schlitt and Bob Hartman meet?

    1. On a mission trip to Guatemala
    2. At a Christian music industry convention
    3. On an airplane
    4. At church

14. Which artist received Christ in a school janitor's broom closet?

    1. Dana Key
    2. Mylon LeFevre
    3. Dallas Holm
    4. Larnelle Harris

15. Which bilingual artist started rapping on the streets of San Francisco as a child?

    1. Toby Mac
    2. Mike-E
    3. Knowdaverbs
    4. T-Bone

16. Which one of these is not a magazine that covered Christian music?

    1. *Jesus Music Monthly*
    2. *CCM Magazine*
    3. *7-Ball Magazine*
    4. *HM Magazine*

<u>Bonus</u>: Fellow Mixtape Theologians crafted these questions for your extra credit.

17. What singer was the first to cover Mark Lowry and Buddy Greene's "Mary Did You Know?" (Sharon Moore)

1. Kathy Mattea
2. Bryan Duncan
3. Michael English
4. Jonathan Pierce

18. What 1997 hit song received both a Dove Award and a Grammy Award, multiple cover versions from secular artists, and a Little Golden Book adaptation? (Nathan Ludwick)

1. Steven Curtis Chapman's "I Will Be Here"
2. Bob Carlisle's "Butterfly Kisses"
3. Amy Grant's "Baby Baby"
4. NewSong's "Christmas Shoes"

19. The English cottage Carman described in "A Witch's Invitation" references which popular 1980s horror movie? (Kylan Savage)

1. *Friday the 13th*
2. *The Gremlins*
3. *Poltergeist*
4. *A Nightmare on Elm Street*

20. Rascal Flatts member Jay DeMarcus was also a founding member of which CCM band? (Dean Deaver)

1. Code of Ethics
2. East to West
3. PFR
4. Daniel Amos

Answer Key (No peeking until the end! WWJD!)

1. c: Mark Stuart
2. d: All of the above
3. a: Eric Champion
4. d: Dakoda Motor Co.
5. a: Plumb
6. b: Racism
7. a: Big Tent Revival's Steve Wiggins
8. d: MxPx
9. a: Trin-i-tee 5:7
10. b: Kentucky Christian College
11. a: Steve Taylor
12. a: Take 6
13. c: On an airplane
14. a: Dana Key (and Eddie DeGarmo is the one who led him to the Lord!)
15. d: T-Bone
16. a: *Jesus Music Monthly*
17. c: Michael English
18. b: Bob Carlisle's "Butterfly Kisses"
19. d: *A Nightmare on Elm Street*
20. b: East to West

DEEP CUT SCAVENGER HUNT

As much as we tried, it was impossible to mention every artist or cultural contribution to 90s Christian culture. To pay homage to a few more, artist Liz King has created a picture scavenger hunt of items left behind in the 90s. Warning: If you don't like puns, you might want to turn the page. Can you find them all?

- 4HIM's puzzle piece
- Five O'Clock People's water bottle
- Acappella's microphone
- All Star United's bright red carpet
- Amy Grant's baby baby
- Anointed's cell phone
- Audio Adrenaline's zombie
- Avalon's maze
- Bible Man's weapon
- Big Fat Jam's feather boa
- Big Tent Revival's big tent
- Bleach's fabric softener
- Bob Carlisle's butterfly kisses

- Bride's wedding veil
- Burlap to Cashmere's basic instruction manual
- Caedman's Call's bus driver
- Carman's rock
- Charlie Peacock's zoo monkeys
- Chasing Furies's rose
- Christafari's soulfire extinguisher
- Cindy Morgan's hearing aide
- Circle of Dust's circle of dust
- Clay Crosse's globe
- Crystal Lewis's counter
- Dakoda Motor Company's surfboard
- Dave Ramsey's wallet
- David Crowder's thank-you note
- dc Talk's flashlight
- Delirious?'s happy heart
- Disciple's dead Easter bunny
- Donnie McClurkin's search light
- East to West's compass
- Eric Champion's vertical reality (VR) goggles
- FFH's big fish
- Five Iron Frenzy's dandelions
- Geoff Moore and the Distance's home-run plate
- Ghoti Hook's banana
- Gotee Brother's sweet tea
- Greg Long's measuring tape
- Grit's grits
- Insyderz's prop gun
- Jaci Valasquez's knee pads
- Jars of Clay's pottery
- John Jonethis's lounge chair
- Johnny Q. Public's body diagram
- Kathy Troccoli's candle
- Kevin Max's black sheep
- Kirk Franklin and God's Property's shoe
- Larry's missing hairbrush

- Living Sacrifice's birth certificate
- Margaret Becker's deep end swim floaties
- Mark Lowry's sugarless cornbread
- McGee and Me's pencil
- Michael Card's poem of your life
- Michael W. Smith's missing person poster
- Miss Angie's eyeball
- Mortification's brutal warfare gas mask
- MXPX's hair gel
- Newsboys's alien
- Nichole Nordeman's wide-eyed drops
- O.C. Supertones's chasing the sunscreen
- Out of Eden's gardening tools
- Patch the Pirate's eye patch
- Paul Wilbur's Star of David
- Petra's hairspray
- PFR's umbrella
- Plankeye's eye injury
- Plumb's plum
- P.O.D.'s receipt
- Point of Grace's bridge
- Prince of Egypt's staff
- Rebecca St. James's praying hands
- Rich Mullins's dulcimer
- Sandi Patty's peppermint patty
- Sarah Masen's all-fall-down bandages
- Seven Day Jesus's barbell
- SFC's house
- Shirley Caesar's salad
- Sixpence None the Richer's father's map
- Smalltown Poets's monkey paw
- Stavesacre's scarecrow
- Steve Taylor's deceased sock
- Steven Curtis Chapman's saddle
- Stryper's 777 (™)
- Susan Ashton's Grand Canyon postcard

- Switchfoot's elevator floor indicator
- T-Bone's assassinating microphone
- Tammy Trent's stethoscope
- The Winans's friendship bracelet
- The W's bowling shirt
- Third Day's tin-foil hat
- Tooth and Nail's broken tooth
- Trin-i-Tee 5:7's pork chops
- Twila Paris's Eiffel Tower
- Wayne Watson's pocket watch
- Wish for Eden's fish bowl
- World Wide Message Tribe's trampoline
- Zilch's Zero

"THAT WAS THEN, THIS IS NOW"

A few years ago, my (Ashley) daughter Ellie discovered one of the "original" reality TV shows, *America's Funniest Home Videos* (*AFV*). She loves it! And, yes, I admit that I like it too. How can you not like cute pets doing ridiculous things? How can you not chuckle at someone getting hit in the head or being nailed in some other random body part (ahem)? Falling off skateboards, people passing out at weddings, and pranks on your spouse are must-see TV!

I remember my family gathered around our TV on Sunday evenings back in the day with no remote control, watching *AFV*. We giggled and cringed, made our cases for the best video of the night, then waited a week for more escapades of pets, pain, and pranks. DVRs and remotes now make things a little easier, and we can binge-watch any season we want. Yet, my family does essentially the same thing that my family did in the 90s—we watch and laugh, spending quality time together. Sure, Bob Saget hosted back then (minus the Olsen twins, "dude"), and Alfonso Ribiero hosts now (minus "The Carlton"). But the show is the same premise it was 30 years ago with new twists here and there.

The idea for this final segment of *Mixtape Theology* came to me after watching *AFV* for 30 years (which has made some of us feel old enough to reach for ibuprofen and arthritis medication). The show recently added a new segment called "That Was Then, This is Now," in which Alfonso presents a video from the 90s, complete with grainy footage and a date stamp from an outdated video recorder. He'll say, "That was then," and show a clip of someone running into a screen door. Then he'll say, "And this is now," and play a new video from the 2020s, in which someone also…wait for it… runs into a screen door.

It truly is amazing how 30+ years ago seems so long ago and yet still like yesterday. And, how in 1990, we thought 1960 was *old*! The music, the styles, the technology, and even the things that people did in church cause us to reflect on the ever passing of time. That got us thinking! What about a version of "That Was Then, This is Now" to complete this mixtape trip of nostalgia?

That Was Then: Teens had "youth groups" and churches had "song directors."

This Is Now: Teens have "student ministries" and churches have "worship pastors." (This would be a good example of ecclesiological evolution!)

That Was Then: Christians often brought big Bibles to church. These Bibles might have a Bible cover with a Jesus fish on it or the person would put stickers on their Bibles and write on them.

This is Now: Christians often don't bring their Bibles to church anymore. But, don't fret. Most of them have the Blue Letter Bible App on their phones, which is amazing! It contains word studies, translation comparisons, and even commentaries. (The problem is that adults and teens alike have the appearance of "looking" spiritual. We all know Mom is on Facebook, and Kinsley the 9th grader is on Instagram! This would be reverse evolution.)

That Was Then: Churches utilized dry ice and water to make smoke for church plays and youth musicals. (Disclaimer: Don't lick dry ice with your tongue, or you will end up on *Rescue 911*.)

This Is Now: Churches utilize smoke machines to enhance worship. (Disclaimer: Smoke machines can be neat, but they neither invoke the Holy Spirit nor do they kill COVID-19.)

That Was Then: In the late 90s, a goatee was the youth pastor's facial hair of choice.

This Is Now: Reformed pastors and youth leaders grow giant beards as they seek to invoke their inner Charles Spurgeon.

That Was Then: WWJD bracelets

This Is Now: WWJD tattoos

That Was Then: The choir wore robes.

This is Now: The worship leader wears skinny jeans and V-necks or shirts two sizes too small, so their large muscles are displayed.

That Was Then: "Left Behind"

This Is Now: "God's Not Dead"

That Was Then: Steven Curtis Chapman was the gold standard for Contemporary Christian Music and songwriting.

This Is Now: Steven Curtis Chapman is the gold standard for Contemporary Christian Music and songwriting. (OK, we know there are different opinions out there, and many great artists exist. Rachel and I just happen to be a little biased toward SCC!)

That Was Then: Men wear suits to church.

This Is Now: Seminary professors wear bowties to chapel.

That Was Then: My cassette and CD collection

This Is Now: My favorite streaming app

That Was Then: Churches showcase annual *Judgment Houses* to scare the community out of hell.

This Is Now: Churches utilize the ever-popular "bouncy houses," yet still reach certain degrees of hell with overcrowded, sweat-saturated, appendage-breaking, non-monitored cesspools of germs and snot.

That Was Then: Red Rover and trust falls, and everyone survived.

This Is Now: "We fired the last youth pastor who played those dangerous Hunger Games!"

That Was Then: Church youth groups formed prayer circles and squeezed the next person's hand if they didn't want to pray. And, everybody peeked!

This is Now: People still peek as they secretly play Fortnite and Minecraft while in Zoom prayer meetings.

That Was Then: dc Talk

This is now: _____

We truly hope that this book has sparked something in you again–that excitement and joy of discovering God's truth in a fresh way. I (Rachel) remember with clarity looking up the Bible verses found in Steven Curtis Chapman's album notes and memorizing those Scriptures, such as Galatians 5:13 from "Remember Your Chains" or John 10:10 from "More to This Life." When I read these verses again as an adult, my mind goes back to those earlier days, and I thank God for those precious times of just Him and me in my room with an NIV Teen Study Bible on my lap and WAY-FM playing in the background.

We may not ever be able to recapture those feelings quite the same way again. That chapter of life is over, and this book is about to end. That feels kind of sad. But, here's the life-giving truth: That which excited us back then is all still true today. As 4HIM stated on their classic *Face the Nation* album, "He never changes!"

In an ever-changing world, He is my hope and guide. He is the Alpha and Omega, the beginning and the end (See Revelation 22:13.). His grace is always sufficient, and His strength is made perfect in our weakness (See 2 Corinthians 12:9.). His mercies continue to be new every morning (See Lamentations 3:22-23.). Salvation by grace through faith has not changed (See Ephesians 2:8-9.).

The sufficiency of God's Word and our need to preach it in season and out of season is still true (See 2 Timothy 4:2.). Indeed, His Word is profitable for teaching, for reproof, for correction, and for training in righteousness (See 2 Timothy 3:16.). God's Word endures (See 1 Peter 1:25.).

Jesus, the Living Word, makes Himself known (See John 1.). We endure when our salvation is in Him (See 2 Timothy 2:8-10.). The world needs to see Him (See Matthew 5:16-17.).

The sanctity of life is as true as it ever has been (See Psalm 139.). Racial challenges and disparity due to sex or economic status still abound, and Jesus is the answer (See Galatians 3:28). Broken and lost people are everywhere, and Jesus comes to save, rescue, reconcile, and justify by His blood (See Romans 5:6-10.). The need for us to engage the culture with the truth of God's Word and the love and grace of the cross continues (See John 17:14-19.).

Jesus is not just the Lord of our lives, *He is life* (See Galatians 2:20.). He loves us, and His cross saves us (See John 3:16.). The Holy Spirit still moves and speaks (See John 16:12-15.).

The commission that Jesus gave us to make disciples has not changed (See Matthew 28:18-20.). The call to love has not changed (See Galatians 5:13-14.). Going to the utmost has not changed (See Acts 1:8.).

Indeed, God is still on His throne (See Psalm 47:8.). In an ever-changing world, a constant exists. That constant is the Father, the Son, and the Holy Spirit (See 2 Corinthians 13:14.).

If we compare the then and the now, I'm thankful that what matters most never changes. So saddle up your horses, all you Jesus Freaks. Jesus is still alright. It is time to let Christ shine! Sure, another time and another place is in our future, but we are not home yet! Luv is a verb, and it is not love until we give it away! Where is our place in this world? It is doing the walk with Jesus! We proclaim that every heartbeat bears His name. I've been crucified with Christ, and yet I live. Not I, but Christ who lives within me!

Thanks to the eternal life in Jesus, "The Great Adventure" is only just beginning. See you on the trail!

"The cassettes get lost and the CDs get scratched but the Word of the Lord endures forever" (1 Peter 1:24, Mixtape Theology version).

WORKS CITED

1. "Heaven in the Real World"

Heiser, Michael S. *The Unseen Realm: Recovering the Supernatural Worldview of the Bible.*
Bellingham, WA, Lexham Press, 2015.

2. "New Way to be Human"

Heiser, Michael S. *The Unseen Realm: Recovering the Supernatural Worldview of the Bible.*
Bellingham, WA, Lexham Press, 2015.

3. "Big House"

Stuart, Mark. *Losing My Voice to Find It: How a Rock Star Discovered His Greatest Purpose.*
Nashville, TN, Thomas Nelson / Nelson Books, 2019.

4. "More Than You Know"

Bridges, Jerry. *Trusting God.* Colorado Springs, CO, NavPress Publishing Group, 2017,
p 295.

5. "The Devil is Bad"

Guthrie, Nancy. *Even Better than Eden: Nine Ways the Bible's Story Changes Everything about
Your Story.* Wheaton, IL, Crossway, 2018, p 33.

Wakefield, Norm. *Equipped to Love*: *Building Idolatry-Free Relationships*. Belverde, TX, Elijah Ministries, 2010, p 26.

6. "Hold Me Jesus"

Farley, Andrew. *The Naked Gospel: The Truth You May Never Hear in Church*. Grand Rapids, MI, Zondervan, 2009, p 205.

> Quote Taken from *The Naked Gospel: The Truth You May Never Hear in Church* by Andrew Farley Copyright © 2009 by Andrew Farley. Used by permission of Harper-Collins Christian Publishing. www.harpercollinschristian.com

Lundgaard, Kris A. *The Enemy Within: Straight Talk About the Power and Defeat of Sin*. Phillipsburg, NJ, P&R Publishing Company, 1998, p 36.

> Quote reprinted from The Enemy Within: Straight Talk About the Power of Defeat of Sin by Kris A.Lundgaard, copyright 1998, P&R Publishing, Phillipsburg, NJ. Used with permission.

7. "Liquid"

Welcher, Rachel Joy. *Talking Back to Purity Culture*. Downers Grove, IL, InterVarsity Press, 2020, p 137.

8. "God"

Augustine. *The Confessions of St. Augustine*. Public Domain. https://www.gutenberg.org/ebooks/3296

Sproul, R.C. *Everyone's a Theologian: An Introduction to Systematic Theology*. Sanford, FL, Ligonier Ministries, 2014, p 91.

9. "The Robe"

Schreiner, Thom. *Faith Alone–The Doctrine of Justification: What the Reformers Taught…and Why It Still Matters*. Grand Rapids, MI, Zondervan, 2015, p 184.

> Quote Taken from Faith Alone–The Doctrine of Justification: What the Reformers Taught…and Why It Still Matters by Andrew Farley Copyright © 2015 by Thom Schreiner. Used by permission of HarperCollins Christian Publishing. www.harpercollinschristian.com

Sproul, R.C. *Everyone's a Theologian: An Introduction to Systematic Theology.* Sanford, FL, Ligonier Ministries, 2014, p 235.

Spurgeon, Charles. "The Lord Our Righteousness." 1861. Public Domain. https://www.spurgeon.org/resource-library/sermons/jehovah-tsidkenu-the-lord-our-righteousness/#flipbook/

10. "Stomp"

Batterson, Mark. *In a Pit with a Lion on a Snowy Day: How to Survive and Thrive When Opportunity Roars.* Portland, OR, Multnomah Books, 2006, p 168.

Bonhoeffer, Dietrich. *The Cost of Discipleship.* New York, NY, Touchstone, 1995, p 193.

Renner, Rick. *Sparkling Gems from the Greek.* Tulsa, OK, Teach All Nations, 2003. pp 37-38.

11. "Crucified with Christ"
(none)

12. "No Condemnation"

Luther, Martin. *D. Martin Luthers Werke: Kritische Gesammtausgabe.* Vol. 5, Weimar, 1883, p 608.

13. "In Christ Alone"

Nee, Watchman. *Sit, Walk, Stand.* Carol Stream, IL, Tyndale House Publishers, Inc., 1977, p 56.

14. "The Great Adventure"

Keller, Timothy. *The Prodigal God: Recovering the Heart of the Christian Faith.* New York, NY, Penguin Books, 2008, p XIX.

Stone, Dan and Gregory, David. *The Rest of the Gospel: When the Partial Gospel Has Worn You Out.* Eugene, OR, Harvest House Publishers, 2000, p 251.

Published by Harvest House Publishers, Eugene, Oregon 97408. www.harvesthouse-publishers.com. Used by Permission.

15. "I'll Lead You Home"

Owen, John. *Of the Mortification of Sin in Believers*. 1656. Public Domain. Chapter XIII. https://ccel.org/ccel/owen/mort/mort.i.i.html

16. "I Surrender All"

Tozer, A W. *The Pursuit of God*. 1948. Public Domain. https://www.gutenberg.org/ebooks/25141

17. "Where There is Faith"

Spurgeon, Charles. "Faith: What is it? How Can it Be Obtained?" 1881. Public Domain. https://www.spurgeon.org/resource-library/sermons/faith-what-is-it-how-can-it-be-obtained/#flipbook/

Strobel, Lee. *The Case for Hope: Looking Ahead with Confidence and Assurance*. Grand Rapids, MI, Zondervan, 2022, p 8.

Quote Taken from *The Case for Hope: Looking Ahead with Confidence and Assurance* by Lee Strobel Copyright © 2022 by Lee Strobel. Used by permission of HarperCollins Christian Publishing. www.harpercollinschristian.com

Strobel, Lee. *The Case for the Real Jesus: A Journalist Investigates Current Attacks on the Identity of Christ*. Grand Rapids, MI, Zondervan, 2009, p 10.

Quote Taken from *The Case for the Real Jesus: A Journalist Investigates Current Attacks on the Identity of Christ* by Lee Strobel Copyright © 2009 by Lee Strobel. Used by permission of HarperCollins Christian Publishing. ww.harpercollinschristian.com

18. "Addicted to Jesus"

Chalmers, Thomas. *The Expulsive Power of a New Affection*. 1825. Public Domain. https://www.monergism.com/expulsive-power-new-affection

19. "God is in Control"

Lloyd-Jones, D. Martyn. *Spiritual Depression: Its Causes and Its Cure*. Grand Rapids, MI, Wm B. Eerdmans Publishing, Co, 1965, p 140.

WORKS CITED

Tripp, Paul David. *Suffering: Gospel Hope When Life Doesn't Make Sense*. Wheaton, IL, Crossway, 2018, p 163.

Quote taken from *Suffering: Gospel Hope When Life Doesn't Make Sense* by Paul David Tripp, Copyright © 2018, pp. 163. Used by permission of Crossway, a publishing ministry of Good News Publishers, Wheaton, IL 60187, www.crossway.org.

20. "Beauty for Ashes"

Spurgeon, Charles. *Morning and Evening*. "August 6." 1865. Public Domain. https://www.heartlight.org/spurgeon/0805-am.html

21. "We Believe in God"

Augustine. *The Confessions of St. Augustine*. Public Domain. https://www.gutenberg.org/ebooks/3296

Hill Perry, Jackie. *Gay Girl, Good God: The Story of Who I Was, and Who God Has Always Been. Nashville*. TN, B & H Publishing Group, 2018, p 190.

22. Hope to Carry On

Turner, Lee. *Discover Your Riches in Christ: They Are Out of This World!* Pigeon Forge, TN Grace Discipleship Ministries and Grace Fellowship International, 2012, p 25.

23. "Jesus Will Still Be There"

Elliot, Elisabeth, and Joni Eareckson Tada. *Suffering Is Never for Nothing*. Nashville, TN, B & H Publishing Group, 2019, pp 7, 12, 15-16.

24. "As It Is in Heaven"

Mohler, R. Albert. *The Prayer That Turns the World Upside Down: The Lord's Prayer as a Manifesto for Revolution*. Nashville, TN, Thomas Nelson, 2018, p 9.

Quote Taken from *The Prayer That Turns the World Upside Down: The Lord's Prayer as a Manifesto for Revolution* by R. Albert Mohler, Jr. Copyright © 2018 by R. Albert Mohler, Jr. Used by permission of HarperCollins Christian Publishing. www.harpercollinschristian.com

Sproul, R.C. *The Holiness of God (25th Anniversary Edition)*. Sanford, FL, Ligonier Ministries, 2010, p 15.

25. "On My Knees"

Forsyth, P.T. *The Soul of Prayer*. 1916. Public Domain. https://ccel.org/ccel/forsyth/prayer/prayer.iv.html

26. "Well, Alright"

Ryle, J.C. "To Whom?" 1880. Public Domain. http://www.tracts.ukgo.com/ryle_to_whom.pdf

27. "Shine"

Bates, Matthew W. *Why the Gospel?: Living the Good News of King Jesus with Purpose*. Grand Rapids, MI, Wm B. Eerdmans Publishing, Co, 2023, pp 63, 68.

"Ask Pastor John: What is God's Glory?" *Desiring God*, 8 May 2023, www.desiringgod.org/interviews/what-is-gods-glory--2

28. "Testify to Love"

"Witness." 3144. *Strong's Exhaustive Concordance*. Public Domain. https://bibleapps.com/strongs/greek/3144.htm

29. "Luv is a Verb"

Chan, Francis. *Crazy Love: Overwhelmed by a Relentless God (Revised and Updated)*. Colorado Springs, CO, David C Cook, 2013, pp 103-104.

Excerpted from Crazy Love © 2008, 2013 by Francis Chan. Used by permission of David C Cook. May not be further reproduced. All rights reserved.

Peterson, Eugene H. *The Message: The Bible in Contemporary Language*. Colorado Springs, CO, NavPress Publishing Group, 2017, 1 Corinthians 13:1-3.

30. "Jesus Freak"

dc Talk and Voice Of The Martyrs. *Jesus Freaks: Martyrs: Stories of Those Who Stood for Jesus: The Ultimate Jesus Freaks*. Bloomington, MN, Bethany House Publishers, 2014, p 8.

WORKS CITED

31. "Consuming Fire"

Pink, Arthur W. "The Attributes of God." 1925. Public Domain. https://www.monergism.com/thethreshold/sdg/attributes_online.html

32. "Under the Influence"
(none)

33. "Open the Eyes of My Heart"
(none)

34. "Another time, Another Place"
(none)

35. "I Will Be Free"

Spurgeon, Charles. "The Beatific Vision." Public Domain. https://www.spurgeon.org/resource-library/sermons/the-beatific-vision

SPECIAL THANKS TO SPECIFIC MIXTAPE THEOLOGIANS

Our community of mixtape theologians are 'da bomb. From serving as beta readers to social media sharers to launch team members and more...you humble us with your support. We were once strangers, but now we are thankful to call you friends. We would like to recognize the following individuals for saddling up and blazing trails on behalf of *Mixtape Theology*.

Adrián Casas
Allison Payne
Andi Soergel
Angie Carroll
Ashley Hale
Brooke Dircksen
David Jarrell
David Tooley
Dean Deaver
DeWayne Hamby
Eric McClanahan
Erik Sellin
Greg Barron

SPECIAL THANKS TO SPECIFIC MIXTAPE THEOLOGIANS

Gretchen Probst
Jamie Nixon
Jason Parker
Jessica Tucker
Josh Balogh
Justin N Holton
Kevin Jewell
Kim Reed Bracey Johnson
Laressa Nordgren
Mark Cheathem
Mary Beth Bernheisel
Matt Davis
Matthew Hawk
Micah Watson
Michelle Nezat
Mindy Boardwine
Olivia Balding
Pete Ford
Rhonda Delph
Rob Canavan
Scott Anderson
Shelley Gorin
Treeva Burris

AUTHORS' THANKS

ASHLEY AND RACHEL WISH TO THANK:

Liz King, you da bomb. You know who's doin' it? Thank you to Kevin McNeese at NRT for making this something more than we could ever do on our own. Thank you, Mac Powell, for your wonderful foreword! Thank you Cameron Frank and Preston Norman at A Frank Voice for your ministry, expertise and heart. Thank you to our church family, White House First Baptist! Thank you to the songwriters, producers, musicians, and artists that created this music that we love so much. Your art has discipled us and changed our lives. Thank you to the Mixtape Theologians who followed us on social media, listened to our podcast, and have become our new friends. Most importantly, thank you to our Savior for being the same - yesterday, today, and forever. Hallowed be Your name.

ASHLEY WISHES TO THANK:

Thank you to my parents for raising me to love Jesus and teaching me how much He loves me. Following Jesus makes all the difference! Thank you, Jerry, my "Paul," who was a Steven Curtis Chapman superfan long before I was and gave me my first CCM cassette upon graduation. You never know how much one small gift of a 4Him tape will shape someone's life. More than the tape, God used you to shape me. Rachel, thank you for allowing me to participate in this project. When you polled people on social media about their interest in a devotional on 90s CCM, I never dreamed my response would lead to me writing it with you. You are a true friend; words cannot express my gratitude for your hard work and dedication. We are a good team! Thank you, Emily, our family's true scholar, and writer, for supporting and encouraging me through this endeavor. You amaze me, and I am the luckiest man on the planet to be married to you. You are my soul-mate! I love you! And to Ellie, if I could pick out one girl in the entire world to be my daughter, I'd choose you every time. You are an amazing Christian young lady; I couldn't be more proud to be your daddy, and I love you!

RACHEL WISHES TO THANK:

Thank you, Aunt Sue, for passing down that SCC CD. It found a good home to say the least. Thank you, Dave Agee. Entwined in my 90s Christian experience, your encouragement has remained with me. Mom and Dad, thank you for nurturing my love for 90s CCM, buying me tickets and cassettes, taking me to my first dc Talk concert while hating it the whole time, creating an entire youth group newsletter just for fun, leading home Bible studies, and for so much more that I can't fit on a page. Ashley, thank you is not enough. My mixtape partner, pastor, and friend, "It's so good to know I've got a friend like u." Thank you, Brad, for being my best friend and the true love worth waiting for. To speak your music language, "I am the luckiest." To my girls, "just between you and me," this book is really for you. I pray you know and love the Lord through this music. Make it your own. Thank you for listening to dc Talk in the car with me and for loving it just as much as I do. It's been so fun experiencing it all again with you. Hey you, I'm into cheeses.

LIZ WISHES TO THANK:

First, I want to thank all the little people... ha ha. Seriously, I first want to thank my Lord and Savior, Jesus Christ! Without Him this means nothing! I want to thank Rachel and Ashley for believing in my work and opening this door of opportunity! My husband Will for getting me my iPad, so I could make my comics digitally and for being awesome! You rock! I love you. My kids for shrugging their shoulders and saying, "I guess it's okay," every time I showed them a comic, and also putting up with me going around the house singing, "You know who's doin it?" I love you. To Jeremie and my brother Liam for helping me edit my grammar. To Sam Iko and Pauline Chambers for being my original audience and encouraging me to continue my comics. To dc Talk for changing my world musically and opening the door to CCM. You will always be my boyz! If you formed a gang I would totally join it!!! To TobyMac for being obedient to God even during the difficult times. You were my Billy Graham. To my mom and dad who laugh at my stupidity. I also want to thank Melanie for always seeing things that other people didn't in my humor. To my friends, I love you. Thanks for loving my interesting personality and my awkward moments.

Peace!

075bab11-aee6-4e05-8572-d42b0fadd1b1R01